STAY IN THE LIGHT

Shelley Elina Williams

authorHOUSE®

AuthorHouse™
1663 Liberty Drive
Bloomington, IN 47403
www.authorhouse.com
Phone: 1-800-839-8640

Published by AuthorHouse   07/28/2012

ISBN: 978-1-4685-9484-3 (sc)
ISBN: 978-1-4685-9485-0 (e)

Library of Congress Control Number: 2012907344

Contents

Acknowledgments

I would like to praise God in the name of Jesus Christ, for guiding mc with the words and strength in writing this book. Without my Lord my savior it would not be. I would like to dedicate this book to my son Darnell W. Adkins and my step son Nathan. They both were struck with illness at a young age. Unable to hold down jobs because of illness. This led to no income. I pray they will trust and believe in Jesus. Who through the Father can change their life and bless them both. He is always there for you. He waits for you with love. Jesus provides spiritual sustenance for a life giving relation with God the Father, the Son, and the Holy Spirit.

Inspiration with a twist

They will help a devil
Before they help an angel

A Blessing From Christ

In the name of Jesus, I send this blessing and my love for him. Accept this blessing in the name of Jesus. For all blessing come through Jesus. Through your faith he gives spiritual currency. And through your faith it will grow and grow in Jesus name. Accept not and judge, get only what you can produce. Glory to Jesus for a King is born. Aman

All Knowing and Powerful

God said I am your God and will take care of you; I made you and will take care of you (Isaiah 46: 4-10). God predicted the outcome of things to come long ago he foretold what would happen in the world. God speak and it will be done, God do not lie he is the truth always. Who other than God can say what will happen in the future, and it is as he said, only God and the Son. God is all knowing and powerful, and he wants you to understand the Word of God. That's why he had the Bible written.

Read the good book and know your God, do not settle for man's word. Know the true Word of God. I believe and know in my heart that this world is our test before judgment. What you do and say in this world will decide your fate by our Lord Jesus Christ. The question is will you go to the light, or will you end-up in the dark. You are making your own choice by what you do and say, so choose very carefully. It means eternal life or the dark of the fire pit forever with Satan.

I pray we all make it to the light were we will live forever. God will save all people who believe in him and his son Jesus. He knows your heart so do not think you can fool God, he is forgiven but he is no fool. You will end-up being the fool, if you think you can fool God. He is an all knowing powerful God. Talk is cheap he knows your truth; God will have the last word. Don't try to use the Lord for your evil deeds, because you will pay today or tomorrow.

The Lord's book "The Bible" is a book of truth and revelation. We are all very special to God he loves us, that's why he created us in his image and likeness. So love him and his son Jesus as they love you. Show the Lord your love welcome him into your life, pray and talk to him. Make Jesus your main friend and brother. You will not be sorry, because anything is possible through your Lord Jesus Christ.

Remember you are loved by God, so if you find no love in mankind go to God. There is always love with our Lord. Remember Jesus Christ paid the penalty for our sins and die on the cross for you to have eternal life with him.

All You Need

Why do people sin? People no longer have any excuse for their sin, they sin just because. If you sinners want out call on Jesus he will send his helper, his Father's Spirit that comes from God (John 15: 26). Jesus died on the cross so your sins could be forgiven by God's Holy Spirit. God only ask that you believe in his son Jesus Christ. Open your heart and let the light of Jesus shine upon you.

Let Jesus manage your suffering and your demons. The Lord can make you forget your suffering and provide for your needs. And if your faith in him is great, he will grant your desires, they will be gifts from God. Your Lord will strengthen you and make you strong. You will feel his Holy Spirit, and he will make your enemy's run. And all you need is faith in your Lord Jesus Christ. Put your trust in Jesus and you will know the truth.

The Father will give you whatever you ask of him, in the name of Jesus (John 16:23). The Father loves you, because you love Jesus and you believed that Jesus came from God. Yes all you need is to believe and trust in God's son Jesus.

Believers

Believers are children of light. Study the prophecy signs. Believers should watch.

Jesus wants us to be watching. Believers should be alert and self-controlled.

Believers should put on faith, love and hope. Believers should know he is our hope, he is coming.

The second coming is our hope in Jesus name.

Just

God is just; he will pay back trouble to those who trouble you. He will give relief to you who are trouble.

He will punish those who do not know God and do not obey the gospel of our Lord Jesus Christ.

He is a God who judges sin, and his judgments are just. Christ return ensures the final judgment.

Read: 2 Thessalonians 1: 5-10.

Blessing From God

Your blessing from God could be great; he would like to make you comfortable. God gives us all things to enjoy. There are people not of God who get mad about your blessings from God. They will try to put a guilt trip on you, but they fail to realize that you are a person that's been blessed by our Lord. They do not realize that when they put God's people down, God will put them down. So I say to you change your ways and step into the light and receive God's blessings.

When you are blessed by our Lord do not let things go to your head. Remember to forgive those who are against you for the Lord will bless you more; you never can have too many blessings. Do not let your possessions change you. Do not let your riches make you arrogant. Take care that your wealth do not make you feel superior to people who do not have it. Do not let your money make you feel like you have power or control over others, we are all God's people, until you yourself refuse to be a person of God.

Power and control belongs to God, our Lord God is in control of everything. Power tends to corrupt people; they begin to let Satan take over their lives. They become arrogant and have no regard for the rights and needs of others. If you are rich stay in the light with Jesus, do good with your wealth. Jesus teaches that you should be rich in good works. You should share with the poor or others in need of your help.

Your wealth was given to you by God, so others can be blessed by your good deeds. Remember your time here on earth is a test before our Lord Jesus Christ, who keeps a book of names for end time. God said love your neighbor as you love yourself; help them in need and God will bless you even more. You will never be poor because you are storing up a good foundation in God's Kingdom by helping others and respecting others with less than yourself.

We as God's people need to stand against arrogance, deception, stupidity, and greed. Stay in the light of our Lord Jesus Christ, and pursue righteousness, faith, patience and love in the name of Jesus. The Lord's light is safe and peaceful; remember God is in control of everything.

Born Again

When your heart is with God, the Lord your God will always forgive you. Jesus wants you to put your faith in him, and believe in him, trust in him. You must show your faith by trusting and believing in him. Pray to him, talk to him, he do hear you.

John 3:1-2 Jesus said, no one can enter the Kingdom of God without being born of water and the spirit. You must be born again, spiritually of the spirit. You must be lifted up in the spirit, so that if you believe in God the Father, the Son and the Holy Spirit you will have eternal life. God loves us so much he gave his only son. So who ever believes in his son, may have eternal life.

Jesus is your savior. Jesus is the light of all people. The light has come into the world to save you. But people love the darkness rather than the light. People love there evil deeds. For those people the fire is hot very hot. Beware people will protect a devil and throw stones at an angel.

Children of God

We are all God's children, but some of us chose to be the child of Satan. They let Satan take over their bodies. Satan knows when he meets a child of God, read Luke 8:26-29. When this demon that was inside a man, saw Jesus he bagged Jesus not to punish him. Jesus asks the demon what was his name. This lets us know that all demons have names.

This is why today you can meet people who are evil, which house evil spirits within. Have you ever met people who never have anything but ugly words to say? When demon spirits know you are a child of God, they hate you and want nothing to do with you, or they only want to hurt you for no reason other than a good laugh.

That's why you must beware, and know who is around you. You must ask the Lord to shield and protect you from demons. Some people, who feel you are of God, will be afraid of you, read Luke 8:34-38. They are afraid of you because they are afraid of God, and do not want to know God. Some portend to know God, but they are afraid to know him and run from the light.

Some people honor God with their words, but not with their heart. They teach words and rules of man; they have clever ways of rejecting Gods words, so they can use their words and rules. Beware there teaching cancels out the Word of God. This will send you to the dark. Stay away from the dark go to the light. Jesus light always shines for you. Read Mark 7:20-23 all evil things that come from inside you make you unclean in our Lords eyes.

Christians Are Tested

We suffer many kinds of trials. Their purpose is to prove that our faith is genuine. Your faith is precious, and it must be tested so that it may endure. You must love him, all though you have not seen him. You must believe in him all though you do not see him. You will receive salvation of your soul, which is the purpose of your faith in him. Read 1Peter 1:7, Romans 8: 28-29. God sees into our hearts. He knows what the thought of our spirit is. The spirit pleads with God on behalf of his people and in accordance with his will. Those whom God has already chosen he set apart to become like his son. He will share his glory with them. If God is for us, who can be against us!

God needs to know if trouble, hardship, persecution, hunger, poverty, or death can separate us from Christ. Temptation is meant to make us good. When Jesus was being tempted by Satan at no time did Jesus use powers to gratify himself. Even when he was arrested, he did not call on angels to rescue him. Even on the cross he prayed for us. Forgive them Father, for they know not what they do. Give yourself unto your Lord, Jesus Christ. For he gave himself for you. Praise his name, as he will praise you unto the Father. For he will take you into his Kingdom. For God is the power the glory forever and ever. In his name I pray.

Cleaning of Babylon

Before the earth can be reclaimed by Jesus it must be cleansed. Read (Revelation 18, 19, 20). God had condemned the prostitute who was corrupting the earth with her immorality. God has punished her because she killed his servants.

The prostitute that is spoken of here is the city Babylon. The city was full of prostitutes and evil men and women. The city was well known with the merchants who were rich and powerful. Merchants came from all nations, to Babylon to do their evil.

Here in the city of Babylon, the blood of the prophets and God's people was found dead. This great city has lost her wealth in one hour by the hand of God. For God has condemned this awful city Babylon, because she even sold slaves human lives.

This was a city of immorality and lust. Be glad for her destruction for God has cleaned house. This was God's second cleaning of the earth, since Noah's Ark. God brought destruction on Babylon because it was corrupting the whole earth.

There will be another big cleaning when Jesus returns to earth. Jesus will defeat the beast (Antichrist) and the false prophets, both will be thrown alive into the lake of fire and sulfur. Jesus will also defeat the armies of the nations that want to destroy his people.

All the armies will be destroyed, by the sword of his mouth. This means Jesus has only to speak the words and it shall be. After he defeats the armies, then comes the cleaning. Jesus will have the birds and other animals eat the dead flesh of the army men and their horses, until all is clean.

This is the third cleaning of the earth and the last. For now Jesus will reclaim the earth, and God will bring a new heaven and a new earth.

David and Goliath

All too often we hesitate to do what we know is right, out of concern for what others might think or say. This is human nature, but if you know it is right to do a certain thing don't be afraid God is always with his people trust and believe in your God almighty. Do not worry what others think or say, this is only Satan trying to pull you from your God. Read 1Samuel, 2Samuel, and 1Chronicles. This will give you great insight on your almighty God.

It reads about four men Samuel, David, Saul, and Goliath. I wanted to call this the good, the bad, the ugly. Samuel and David would be the good, Saul would be the ugly, and Goliath would be the bad. Just having a little fun with it. The reading is very adventuress everyone loves the story about David and Goliath so will you. This reading teaches us not to judge people by their outside physical stature and appearance, but look at what's in a person's heart.

Believe it or not that is how God picked David to be King. Our Father God looks at what is in your heart, not at your birth suit. This reading will teach you a lot about being hostile and jealous. Jealousy is not a good human trait. It's too bad we have to live among this foolishly morally wrong human trait; it's almost like being a bully. God was pleased with David and blessed him well; this made Saul jealous and fearful. Saul was so jealous of David he order his death. Not to go into the story.

I just wanted to show how ugly and dangerous jealousy can be. It can only come from the darkness of the evil one. First remove yourself far from this evil, and pray to the Lord your God to remove this evil demon from your life and let the Lord's light shine on you. Through God David was a great king, but he also was a human being with weakness. David was a sinner before God.

David openly sought God's forgiveness for his sin, and God forgave him. The difference between Saul and David was Saul made excuses to God and pretended all was right between him and God. You must ask the Lord for his forgiveness and be honest with God and others about your sin. Yes David was a great King, but there will be another king even greater without sin. Can you guest who he is; yes Jesus Christ is the only living descendant of David. And Jesus will be the next great King to rule God's Kingdom.

Descendants of Noah's Sons

Two years after the flood, God told Noah's sons to take their family's and go fill the world with their off springs. They walked around for a while, and then they all came together in a city called Babylonia. All the people spoke one language. The people said to each other let us settle here in this land, and let us make bricks and build us a city. Then we can make a name for ourselves, and let us not scatter over the earth.

God came down from heaven to see what they have built. The people thought they no longer needed God. So God mix-up there language so they could not understand each other. And then God scattered them all over the earth with different language and race. This is how different nation and language came about. Do not ever think you do not need the Lord, you will soon find out different.

After the flood all the nations of the earth were descended from the sons of Noah. Noah sons are the ancestors of all people on earth. God just made us different so you will always need him. This means we are all one in the same; we are all connected to each other. That's why God wants you to love your neighbor as you love yourself. Read Genesis 10, 11, and 12.

Our Lord God would like it if we would learn to love all people as one people, because we are all the same, we are all kin like it or not. Our Lord God would love it if we would learn to love each other without the put downs, name calling, fighting, and bulling each other we all have the same God. There is only one God and he said we are kin; he made us in his image. If you love God you would love all people.

Do You Know Him

Do you know him? Have you read the gospel of Jesus Christ? A good Christian to our Lord, do not judge others. Who are you to judge God's people? Our Lord Jesus will judge both the living and the dead. Live spiritually with Jesus in your heart and do not live for things on this earth.

But set your mind on things that are above in God's house. God wants you to obey his commandment, love thy neighbor as you love thy self. This means to love every one of all races. You must know and believe that Jesus died and rose again, because your God almighty will also raise you.

God ask that you be patient and wait on his son. If you are righteous in your life, then you know you are born of him, and shall share eternal life with him. Until then we are to live in love of every one. Our Lord will return to earth at the end time. I pray that you have not defied your Lord.

If you deny your Lord he will deny you. Jesus victory is assured by the Father. Jesus has undisputed authority over all things. So stay in the Light.

Do You Love Him

You look for love there is none.
He gave his Son, for your love.
You look for warmth there is none.
You look for kindness there is none.
He gave you love, He loves you.
You do not love him back.
He still waits for your love.
He will wait till the end.
Will you love him then?
His love is strong.
Your love is weak.
He will give you strength, he will give you life.
Will you love him now, will you love him later?
He will love you always now and later.
He loved you in the beginning.
He will love you today and tomorrow.
He will love you till the end.
Will you love him then?

End Time

Everyone in the world today is blessed; you are blessed because you will not have to live through the end time or the Tribulation period. This is when the Antichrist and the False Prophet will rule the world. Thank God for this blessing because it is a big blessing. If you are not a rich person at end time. Your life will always be in danger. You will not be seen as a human, you will be treated as an animal.

People will not be able to live and play in the open, people will have to always hide. Because people will be caught and sold for money. They will be caught and entrapped to work for the rich, and they will not get paid. If they are no longer useful they will be dispose of. People will not be able to trust anyone, your own will turn you in to save themselves.

The closer it get to the return of Jesus, things will be very grey and dark. The global markets will crash, banks will shut down, all business will go bankrupt, and stocks will be worthless. Billions of people will be out of work, people will lose any money they had in the bank. There will no longer be any kind of money. The world financial meltdown will be a million times worse than any the world has ever had. People will go wild and soon be living like animals with no ware to turn for help.

People will kill each other for their everyday needs. Mankind will be lost without God. Humans will no longer be human. God has taken his Holy Spirit away; God has removed his church from the earth and left us to do it alone. And we think we do not need God. I am here today to say I need God always. I look for my Lord to show me the way; I look for him to easy my pain. I look for God to open doors for me; I look for God to protect me from the evil one. I look for my Lord to shield me from my enemy's.

I look for God to wake me every morning and lead my day. Yes I do need God. The end time will be wicked and evil; people will live in this sinful time until the return of Jesus Christ.

Eternal Wealth

Your life here on earth is temporary; everything on this earth is temporary. When you leave this world only your souls will enter heaven. No earthly thing will enter not money, homes, furniture, toys, or anything. When your souls go to heaven God will give you new bodies, new pure bodies, and you will know who you are. Read what Ecclesiastes 5:10-28 has to say about money.

In God's new world you will have permanent eternal wealth. The money you get in this world is a gift from God he gives you, the power to make money and enjoy it. We as humans have disconnected from reality. We lack understanding and knowledge of the coming times or we just chose not to know. God's Word is a warning to us, but we are not getting it. So read the good book and learn.

God's Word was given to you by God your Father, who would love to share his world with you, come into his light and live. It's time to wake up, do not sleep in the dark stay sober and watch; time is moving. Read (Romans 13:11) (1Thessalonians 5:6) (1Chronicles 12:32) and (Matthew 16:3). Things are changing fast; time is changing and running fast. Time is running like the internet, it is rebooting and updating its self-right before our eyes.

A rapid change today calls for our urgent need to find Jesus and stay in his light. Time is computing its software and has upgraded the financial world and the economy to were the hard drive is too hard to comprehend. We need to find the truth, we need to know the truth, and Jesus is the truth. Follow Jesus and your journey will be meaningful.

The national and the international nations are slowing being combined; we will soon have a global government that wants to have one currency for the whole world. Sorry I cannot get into this, but this will be another big change for us all. I can only say walk with Jesus and stay in the light, the truth is in Jesus light. In (Proverbs 28:20, 22) said a man with an evil eye hastens after riches, and does not consider that poverty will come upon him.

Proverbs 63:9-10 say honor the Lord with your possessions, and with the first fruits of all your increase; so your barns will be filled with plenty, and your vats will overflow with new wine.

Faith

Have faith, don't be against yourself. There are already enough people against us. Everyone has fought.

Keep your shoulders back and hold your head high. Focus on the good things about yourself. Put your faith in Jesus Christ. Ask Jesus to come into your life and guide you. Repent your sins unto your God.

Have faith in Jesus and know without question that he will guide you. Your blessings come from your faith in God; you cannot fake it, because he knows your heart and thoughts.

God will know if your faith is genuine. Always talk to Jesus about your life, and thank him when he blesses you. God made us all weak, so he can use us to show you his power. God does not judge you and he will always forgive you. Jesus just wants you to have faith in him. He wants you to believe in him, and trust in him. You must show God your faith, by just knowing he will answer your prayer. You must trust and believe. If God do not hear your prayer, it is because of your sins that separate you from God.

Always pray and repent you sins in the name of Jesus. Put your faith in the Lord your God, in the name of the Son Jesus. He is waiting on you; he knows you are not perfect.

He made you weak so that you will come to him. Make God your Lord and Savior, in the name of Jesus. God can and will move mountains for his children. Jesus is waiting for you. You must find him, and make him part of your everyday life.

Faith in God

Society can be unfair you can give it all you have, and they will limit you when you know you can do more. Remember what count is how God can enable you. When God opens a door for you no one can close it. So put your faith in God. Remember the Lord could have other plans for you later, just never give up your faith in God and he will not give up on you. As they say good things come to them who wait.

Judges 6-7 tells about a weak man who always obeyed God and through God he ended up being the strongest man in the end. This is why you never ever give up on God; your faith must be true. Another good reason is to insure you make it to God's Kingdom. In Revelation it describes the Holy City it sounds so great. Walls made of jasper, the city made of gold, plus other walls made of all kinds of precious stones, sapphire, emerald, onyx, carnelians, yellow quartz, beryl, topaz, chalcedony, turquoise, amethyst, and pearls.

The tree of life will bear fruit twelve times a year, once each month. And then there's the river of life we will drink from. God will provide for all our needs, nothing that is impure will enter the city. I don't know about you but this sounds good to me! Remember it's your chose were you go from this life, the truth is in the light. The light is in Jesus, so stay in the light of our Lord. Have faith and pray, now is the time to save yourself go to Jesus.

Fallen World

The word became flesh and lived among us. We felled and know his glory was of the Father. God was born a human; in the person know as Jesus of Nazareth. God said now I am a man. Now I am human. God came to us as Jesus, in the simplest form, as an infant. If we deny Jesus is God, we deny the essence of Christianity. The world over looked Mary's little lamb, and it still does.

Jesus lied in a manger and wept, after he was born. It is one of the sad signs of our fallen world. As humans, the first sign we give to show that we are alive is to cry. It is to this fallen world that Jesus came. Not a world without tears. Jesus came so that the Father will take away the tears and sins of man. Read (Luke 2: 21, Leviticus 12: 3) Gods law called for a boy child to be circumcise on the eighth day after his birth. In Luke 2: 21 Jesus had a circumcision on the eighth day after his birth.

The procedure was usually performed by the father of the child, even if it was the Sabbath. This was ok with God. Jesus is the light. The word is the source of life. Light shines in the darkness, the light is Jesus. Believe in him and his light will shine. The only Son who is the same as God. Those who do evil hate the light and will not come to the light. They do not want their evil deeds to be known. Whoever believes in the Son has eternal life.

First Pains

Jesus came to give his life to set people free from sin. In Mark 3:35 Jesus said whoever does the will of God is my family. Jesus talked about getting close to the end of time. He said these things are like the first pains of child birth, read Mark 13: 5-8. Jesus said you will hear the noise of battles close by and news of battles far away. Countries will fight each other. Nations will attack one another. There will be earth quakes everywhere.

Just watch the world, the whole world, not just your world. For the world's birth pains are large, and your world is small. Mark 13: 24-27 gives a small clue it said the Son of Man will appear after the first birth pains. It also says the sun will grow dark, the moon will no longer shine, and the stars will fall from heaven. Then the Son of Man will appear. I believe we are now having the first birth pains, but that's me. What do you believe?

Jesus does not tell us how long between each pain, or how many birth pains there will be. I guess if he did we would be able to predict the end of time. I would say it is good for us that only God knows the time. I do believe he is giving us lots and lots of time to change, because he would readily love for us to change and stop the end to come. For God loves each and every one of us.

Follow My Foot Steps

I live my life a foot step behind Jesus. I do my best to follow. Our father took my hand and led my way. I heard his voice say turn the other cheek, for verges is mine. I heard Satan say he could not stand me, for I turned the other cheek. Every time I stood Satan up, my Lord would bless me. The more Satan pulled, the more I turn my check. The more my Lord blessed me. So many blessings I never ask how. For my trust was in my Lord.

Who I know all things were possible. I heard Satan ask how she does that. I would smile with my Lord and turn my cheek to hear his sweet voice. As I follow his footsteps. I saw wonders you would not believe. Things I could not share with unclean souls. I turn the other cheek, because I know some day I would readily be home. That is the day of my celebration.

From Rich to Poor

God had seven letters send to seven different churches. Read Revelation chapters 2, 3. The seventh church was rejected by God, because they thought they no longer needed God. They said they were wealthy and have need for nothing. So God said he would vomit them out of his mouth. Because they were rich and had no use for God. In Revelation 3: 15-17 God said he would make them miserable, poor and blind.

I tell you if you are rich never ever think you don't need God. A person's life can change in one day from rich to poor. This has happen to so many people in our economy today, and it is still going on. No one knows what tomorrow will bring. So never think you are above others, because you can fall and break your leg just like any human. This is to say you are only human with no magic powers.

So many people are living a false life because of a job title or more schooling or special letters behind their name. People have a false sense of things or of life. God's plans are at work now and every day, we people of today are still blessed because God has not removed his Holy Spirit from the world. When and if he does the world will be lawless and full of evil and we will be under the order of the Antichrist.

There will not be enough faith in the world to bring God's grace back. Evil will be worldwide without God's Holy Spirit no one will be safe. People them self will turn into human demons, doing whatever comes to their mind. The Antichrist will reward them for their evil deeds. All true Christians will have to hide in fear for their life. Christians will have to live this way until Christ, Jesus returns with his angles, to take back his world.

We are moving faster and faster toward this lawless time, the clock is ticking louder and louder. Can you hear it, can you see it, can you feel it, open your eyes and watch. I say to you all, act now find faith in our Lord Jesus. Open your heart and find him, he is waiting for your trust, waiting for your love. Jesus is everywhere where ever you are Jesus is there, just call on him. He does not live in one place he lives in all places, you only need to invite him into your heart and he will come.

Get to know your Lord read his words; hear his words know him as he knows you. Our time is short, his time is forever. He will be there forever just for you.

God Accepts You

God accepts each and every one of us. So do not let evil defeat you, instead conquer evil with good (Romans 12:21). You must find the Lord's light and let the Holy Spirit guide you. Accept one another as Christ has accepted you, and praise God for his mercy. Because God can take you out any time he wants, but he loves us so he has mercy on us, in hopes that we will change and come to him.

We all will stand before God to be judged by him. So why do you pass judgment on others? Who are you to judge? Why do you despise other believers? On judgment day everyone will kneel before the Lord, and everyone will have to give an account to God. Judge not but judge yourself first. God's Kingdom is for the righteous. You much bring peace to one another, and strengthen each other.

Do not condemn yourselves with insults that you use on others. If you are of God, and you feel guilty after you do something, then you know it is wrong, and you should make it right, your Lord is watching. If you do wrong and know it is wrong, and do not want to make it right, then you are of the evil one. May the Lord have mercy on you. Without God's mercy you would not be. Praise and thank God every day.

Accept one another as God has accepted you. One of God's commandments is do not desire what belongs to someone else. Because through Jesus Christ,your desires can come true. Where is your faith? Another commandment is love you neighbor as you love yourself (Romans 13: 9-10), because if you love others you will never do them wrong. So watch what you do and say to others.

Because what is said and done to others, is also said and done to your Lord. Good things are of God. Do unto others as you would want other to do unto you. Are you prepared to stand before God? Your Lord and savior Jesus Christ is your salvation. The clock is still ticking, go into the light before the clock stops and stay in the light. Time is moving fast.

God in America

I am an American, there was a time these words made me feel proud. When I read the bible I could tell our laws and rules came from the Almighty God. America was a blessed nation, but I now think God's blessings are short if any at all. We now cannot display the Ten Commandments in public, we cannot read the bible in public, and I now hear talk about removing the words "Under God" from the Pledge of Allegiance.

My question is, are we now ashamed of God? The way I see it the praise we gave God, we turned around and took his praise back. If we do not live under God, who then do we live under, think about it. Because if you are not for God, then you are for Satan. For me this explains why people are so different today. No one can trust anyone any more, families hate each other, and people want to control and hurt each other.

If you want blessings from God, then make God your priority, work with God! In Genesis 12:1-3 God promised to bless those who bless Israel. America has blessed the Jews and God did bless America. Now America has forgotten where their blessings came from. I say America now needs to go back to the table and think about what God wants; greed is the root of all evil. I would prefer to have God on my side.

Thanksgiving is a day when families should get together for God, it is a day to thank God each year for the blessings you have received from him. Thanksgiving is to offer thanks to the Almighty God. America was born a Christian nation, thank God our money still reads" In God We Trust", this too may end soon. We have put God on the back burner, and our blessings are going up in smoke.

His light shines no more, bring God back to American! I ask myself, what did our nation do to disappoint God? Did we sin before God, and can it be fixed? Were we disloyal, did we degrade God; were we too corrupt or too greedy? I pray for our nation, that we find the light of Jesus and find our way back to God. For God is true always and forever.

God Is

God is a God who keeps his promises
God is a God who hears the prayers of his people
God is a God who responds to his people suffering
God is a God who will deliver his people
God is a God who provides for his people
God is a God who will free his people
God is a God who gives just punishment
God is a God who is always present
God is a God who is there for you
God is a God who loves you
God is a God who blesses the obedient
God is a God who lives forever
God is a God who gives eternal life
God is a God who is in control
God is a God who protects his people from evil spiritual
    powers

God accepts people who trust him, and then he helps them.
Miracles are possible because God exists.
People are not sinners because they do wrong; they are
sinners because they choose to do wrong!
Let them without sin throw the first stone.

God's Love

God is waiting, God loves you. God loves all people. God loves the good, the religious people, and the God fearing people. God also loves the skeptics, the God haters, the pagans, and the evil doers.

God loves the world. God is waiting for you to love him back. He is waiting for you to love his son. God is waiting for you to believe in his son Jesus Christ. God is waiting for you to change your evil ways. God is waiting for you to come unto him. Give your heart unto the Lord your God. Receive unto yourself the love of God, so that he will receive unto you. God loves you. God is waiting for you. Show God your love for him. Obey his laws. Love one another as God loves each of you. For God is love, God is good. Let us thank God for our being.

God's Time

God works in his own time, not our time. God is faithful to us all though we may not always see it. God will avenge all evil that has been done. We may think we have gotten away with our wicked deeds, because he works in his time, so you think there is no God. So you say I can do and say whatever I want. But just know your time will come. People think how can one God be everywhere all the time. That is an easy question if you every read God's Word. You would know the good news.

You would know about the army of angels that live in heaven and may be walking this earth among us. Now think about how you yourself got on this earth if the almighty God had not made it, you would not be here. Give God praise because praise is due. You would know about God's mercy. You would know about his Holy Spirit that protects us. You would know about God's grace that keeps the most evil one from taking over the world.

When the time comes for God to remove his grace from the world, you will bag for his good grace to stay and protect you from the man of sin. Because his evil will be too great to bear. Question our Lord not but bag for his forgiveness, because your wicked sinful ways will not last forever.

He Is

He is the Alpha and the Omega. The beginning and the end. The first word and the last word. He is the word. Who is and who was, and who is to come. The almighty God, he is the Lord of all. He has power over all things. Give him the glory he deserves.

Jesus said "I am coming as a thief". This means the coming of Jesus will be a surprise. This is a reference to the coming of Jesus at the end of the Tribulation Period (the end of our time). Not the Lord's time, God do not end he is forever.

Help Us Lord

Lord help us, 911 came then the war. People feel unsure of them self. These things have changed us. Then our jobs go under, we can barely heat our homes. We can't keep gas in our cars. Lord we wonder can we feed our self's, can we feed our children. Clothes and food go up twice a year. Our income is getting smaller and smaller every year.

I need insurance on my home and car, plus on myself and my kids. Lord help me how will I pay it? How will I pay my house note, how will I pay my rent? Lord tell me, will me and my children freeze to death? But I must keep the heat down. I tell myself some heat is better than none, Lord help us all.

Lord how will we survive, Lord will we survive? My Lord I know not what to do, I know not were to go. Lord, tell me will I have to live under my pouch, will I have to keep warm in a sewer? Lord Jesus help me, Lord help us all. Jesus we need you, we need you today. We need you tomorrow, we need you now. Please, help us Lord.

Helplessness

Today many people are feeling helpless, but we can do nothing about what is going on, and what we see in the world today. Do not worry yourself about it; just get yourself right with Jesus. The older people are remembering how good it was in the day. The younger people seem to be doing the things the world is doing, it's like they are trying to be like the world.

I know that statement do not make much sense, but that's my opinion what's yours, because I find the young people today untouchable with a very hard shell. People will need to learn to come to gather as times get worse. I remember a great story I heard some years ago about the great depression. How all the families from the block would set up a long table on the side walk, and each house would cook one or two dishes of food, and at seven pm the whole block would bring their food and eat to gather.

They did this so no family on their block would go hungry, each house hold would bring what they had or could bring. And on the weekend they would do breakfast and dinner. People were friendly then, today people are afraid of their neighbors. I always say were there's a will there's a way. In order to make it in the coming times, people will need to put their heads to gather and love their neighbors as they love them self, this is one of Gods commandments. Plus two heads are better than one.

So bring Jesus into your life. Ecclesiastes 11:2 say give a serving to seven, and also to eight, for you do not know what evil will be on the earth. When people stand to gather before God, he will give courage and strength to get through whatever you need to go through. So always call on Jesus and know he is there for you. Put your trust in God and see the light of God's blessings. If you love the Lord your God his light will shine for you.

Whenever you feel helpless think of Jesus, he die so you will have a true life in his Kingdom to come, for all who believe and receive him into their heart. If you trust the Lord Jesus Christ you need not fear the pressures of the world. Put your faith in Jesus he will meet your needs. He will put light into the darkness. In (2Corinthians 9:8) and (Philippians 4:19) say God is able to make all grace abound toward you, that you, always having all sufficiency in all things.

So do not give up, look to God for direction if you believe and trust in Jesus you will not be lost, you will know which way to go. So trust in your Lord Jesus Christ.

How Could They

Jesus, how could they not love you? How could they not believe? How could they not have faith?

Jesus, how could they not know? How could they not see? How could they not feel?

Jesus, how could they not hear? How could they not learn? How could they not seek?

Jesus, how could they? How could they?

I Am Home

I pray and trust my Father's will. I look beyond earth's dark shadows. I do not stand idly; there is still work to do. There is still work waiting for me. Do it now while life remains. When that work is completed I shell rest in Jesus arms as he lead me home. All the angels were glad to see me come. They welcome me and said you are now happy at home. Yes I am home at last thank God, I am home.

All the pain and grief is over. I am now at peace forever. Safely at home in heaven at last. I am home in heaven, so happy and bright. There is perfect joy and beauty in this everlasting light. I now have no doubt no worry, home at last, home at last. Thank God I'm home at last.

I Cry

I cry for the world, I cry for them, I cry for me. I cry, I cry, I cry because they do not know. I cry because they do not see. I cry because they are blind unto you my Lord. They do not know your love. They do not know you. They do not feel you. I cry for them, I cry for me.

We need your Holy Spirit to surround us and guide us. May we receive your holy grace and save our souls. I cry because time is close. I cry because, they do not fear, I cry because they do not see. I cry because they do not know, you put it in our hands, to in brace you or not. You do not force us, you give us time. I cry because our time is running out. I cry because our time is close.

I cry because they are blind, when will they see. Will they see you or not. Will they hear you or not. Are we doomed to enter the dark? Will we see the light? Or will we burn forever. The light is good, the light is life, and the light is you my Lord. The light is forever. I cry for you and me. I cry, I cry.

I Have a Plan

A person once told me they do not make plans, they just say God willing. I told them it is good that you say if God's will. But you cannot live in this world without making a plan. If you go see a Doctor you made a plan, doctors see people by appointments so you made a plan to see the doctor. If you say I'm going to mop this floor to day you are making a plan to get your floor moped. God loves for people to make plans.

Because God wants us to take care of his world and we cannot do this without making a plan. If people didn't make plans, rules, or laws, we would be running around like wild bulls ramming into each other. This is why God rules! our first rules, laws, and plans came from our Father God. The good book itself has God's plan that tell us about the past and the future. God has already plan out the world's future. Believe it or not God's plan is coming.

And there is nothing we can do to stop it, because all people are sinners. I believe the only way that God would even think about changing his plan, is that all nations and all people must stop fighting each other and find Jesus, and go into his light. And all people in the whole world must learn to love one another as the Lord loves us. Until then God's plan is ongoing, whether you like it or not.

The good Lord knows people are sinners and his plan will be done. This is a sample of how man will take their own believes and try to put it off on others. Always read the good book and you will know what the Lord wants of you. Follow no man; follow only the Lord's Word.

Jesus Is Coming

Do you know why the bible tells us to keep watching the sky? Because with the return of Jesus different things will happen as he returns to earth. After the tribulation the sun will be darkened and the moon will not give off its light, then the stars will fall from heaven and heaven will be shaken. Now with all this going on, you cannot miss or not know that Jesus is coming, the bible say we all will see him.

Jesus will be coming to conquer his world and do away with Satan and sin. When Jesus come he will not come alone, all his saints and all the people who were ruptured will come with Jesus. They all will participate in the battle for Jesus to reclaim and rule the world. The saints are not the only ones who will come with him. The angels of heaven will also come to battle with Christ, Jesus.

After the big battle Jesus will sit on his throne and rule over the earth. And his believers will have eternal life and peace. For a new world will come with a new ruler, the King of Kings Jesus Christ. And so shall the Lord be glorified, he will rescue his righteous from the wicked and bring judgment where it belongs. Christ will now set up his Kingdom on earth, and all shall be well, in the light of Jesus.

Life

Do you ever just sit back and think about life. Life in general or maybe, just your life. May be your child hood or your first date. If you think about it there is a lot to life. But, I always thank god I have a life. Here are some of the things I think about.

Life is here, life is gone.
Life is fun, life is sad.
Life is hard, life is easy.
Life is beautiful, life is ugly.
Life is kind, life is mean.
Life is good, life is bad.
But that is life.
The life you and I know comes only once.
But life with Jesus is forever.
I love you Jesus for you have been my life.

Listen

There are people who listen to the word with closed minds. They have built around their hearts a comfort zone of religious habits. The Lords words never sink in, because man cares more about his believes and habits, then the holy word.

There are people who look like they are listening to the word, but they fear Gods words. They have stubbornness and hidden resistance. They are afraid to believe the true word. It might disturb the comfy spiritual status quo of their shallow faith. They do not grow by the word, growth stops and faith disappears.

There are people who listen, who is genuinely receptive of the word. The listener takes root and start to grow. But the listener is distracted, anxiety, the seduction of wealth and the world's vanities set in. There is no growth, they no longer listen.

There are people who have a responsive, teachable mind and Gods word sink down deep and take root. Their hearts grow and produce fruit. No one or anything can choke out Gods word. Resistance to change is displaced by Kingdom of God values. The Holy Spirit will show in this person through their values, lifestyle, priorities, and personal relationships.

Read: Mark 4: 15-19
          Mark 13: 20-21
          Matthew 13: 19-22
          Luke 8: 13-14

Live For Jesus

Live for Jesus, for he die for your sins, so you my share your life with him. Stay ready for Jesus return. Live a pure and holy life. Use your common sense, you know right from wrong. The grace of God that brings salvation has appeared to all men, so you know what's right. Do not have worldly lusts, live godly and righteously. In (Matthew 5:44) Jesus said Love your enemies, and bless those who curse you.

Do good to those who hate you, and pray for those who spitefully use you, and persecute you. Do not give up your new home with our Lord Jesus. Yes life is hard and people are evil, but remember life is just a test, find Jesus and he will carry you through. Follow his light to salvation, and know at the end of the rainbow there is life with Jesus. A new life no pain, no sorrow, no hate, only happiness in paradise. Live for Jesus, and he will give you true life. Please read:

Revelation 1:7, Revelation 19:11-21
1Thessalonians 4:13-18
1Corinthians 15:20-51
Matthew 5:44

Lord Give Us Courage

Father we ask in the name of Jesus, give us courage and hope. Lord give us strength and courage to get through are days. Protect us from the wicked and evil that walks our streets. Lord we ask that you keep us safe. For only you Jesus is our source of peace. I pray we keep peace among ourselves. For without the grace of God we would perish. Without the peace of God, we would be unsure of our salvation. For the source of grace and peace is the eternal God.

When you believe God is there for you, no evil source can stop you. He is a God that can do anything. He will give you courage to face the evil one. God ask that you believe in his son Jesus Christ, trust in him and rely on him, adhere to his word. Call upon the son of God. Never mine Satan he will always be there trying to stop you. Have courage believe in the Son of God, and you will have strength to stand before Satan and blow him away.

Marriage

Marriage is intended to be permanent, together forever. Most law's that God made man has changed them to fit what he want them to be. Be careful try not to do that. That's why God had the bible written, so you can read and find out what he said. Not what man said, seek and you shell find.

Matthew 19: 7-9 Jesus said, Moses gave the people permission to divorce their wives, not God. Divorce was never commanded by God! Divorce was permitted by man (Moses). Matthew 19: 9 Jesus made an exception for divorce in cases of sexual immorality or spiritual infidelity. Ephesians 5: 28-33 men should love their wife just as they love their own bodies. A man, who loves his wife, loves himself. Every husband must love his wife as himself, and every wife must respect her husband.

Malachi 2: 13-16 God was angry with his people because he know they have broken their promise to their wife to stay together and be faithful. Plus that promise was made before God. God said he hate divorce. Like Adam and Eve, one man one woman. Adam's wife Eve was made from his rib by God, (Genesis 52: 21-25). Matthew 19:5 God said a man shell leave his Father and Mother and unite with his wife, and the two shell become one. No human being should separate what God has joined together.

God put one man and one woman together. But polygamy was permitted and existed in the first century, but this was never Gods ideal. This was permitted by man.

Millennium Years

Millennium Years is the day of Jesus, or a period of one thousand years. This is the time when Jesus will live on earth with us. It will begin right after Jesus imprisons Satan. Following the return of Christ on earth. The Lord Jesus shall be King over all the earth. You may ask when will Jesus Christ come, only God knows that. The bible tells that the Armageddon is what will trigger Jesus to come back.

The Armageddon will be the last war on earth between all the nations. I believe this war will be in Jerusalem, God's home the place that God loves. The Armageddon war will be started by the Antichrist. This is when Jesus will come to defeat Satan, and when he do defeat Satan this will be the end of the Tribulation age (Revelation 20:1-3). Then the new age will begin the Millennium age.

This is a special time, because Jesus will live among us with his saints and all the good Christians that kept their faith (Revelation 7:13-14) and (Revelation 20:4). The bible tells us that Jesus will live with us for a thousand years (Revelation 20:4-6). For ten centuries Jesus will rule over the entire world. And all Christians will stand before Jesus to be rewarded for their deeds on earth. Read (Romans 14:10) (2Corinthians 5:10) and (Isaiah 40:10).

There are a number of places in the bible where Jesus tells us about the rewards he will bring. (Matthew 16:27) (Revelation 22:12) and (Luke 12:32) there may be more. We will not have to worry about anything during the thousand years (Millennium). Because God will provide for us in abundance, the entire world will be a paradise. We will live the life that God always wanted for us, before Eve eat from the Tree of Knowledge. How great it will be because we kept our faith.

At the end of the thousand years God will release Satan from his prison (Revelation 20:2-10). When I read this I wanted to know why, he would release the evil one when things are going so good. Happy to say I found my answer. Jesus will let Satan go to kill him for good after this; sin will be gone for good. Then God will bring a new earth from heaven as promised (Revelation 3:12 and 21:2).

You may ask why a new earth, because Jesus want a fresh new earth that has not been touch by sin or by Satan, can you blame him! In Luke 1:31-33 tells us that Jesus Kingdom will not end that means all God's people will live forever. Isn't that worth being a person of God? Jesus taught his disciples to pray for his Kingdom to come, you also should pray for Jesus kingdom to come see (Luke 11:2, 4).

Our Father in heaven. Your Kingdom come. Your will be done, on earth as it is in heaven. Deliver us from the evil one. Go to Luke to get the whole prayer. Let me mention that the word millennium is not in the bible, the bible only uses the words a thousand years, but millennium means one thousand years.

My Brother

My dear brother Jesus, I thank you for covering me with your cloak in my time of need. For I have feared no man. For I know you are with me. You protect me from the evils of the world. You have been my brother, my sister, my friend. For you are always there. You stood up to the evil dark spirits that would like to destroy me, you keep me safe. I have seen their fear of you and me, because I am of you, my Lord.

They do not know why they hate. For they hate for no reason at all. You have guided me in the art of turning the other cheek. I have seen them run the other way, when they feel your holy spirit around me. Their tongues are like the evil one, sliders like a snake. When my brother Jesus raises his arms into the air, he catches the words of Satan. Then the tongue sliders back under the rock it came from. For my love and faith for you is of you. I know your love and protection of me comes from the Fathers light. For I am brighten with my brothers light.

My Prayer for Me and You

I send this out to all, in the name of Jesus.

My prayer for you and your family. I pray God look mercifully upon you.

May the Father be gracious according to your needs.

Dear Father preserve their life and relieve them of pain, and restore them to good health and strength.

I pray you put them in your fatherly care. Forgive them all their sins. So they may be at peace with you.

Lord I ask that you grant this prayer through your blessed son our savior Jesus Christ.

Love to all through Jesus Christ.

Aman

My Trip to Heaven

My trip started with a common car accident. My head hit the steering wheel. I was knocked un-conscious. In this state I travel in a long tunnel, floating up and up. It was so calming and relaxing. I felled the utmost happiness. Looking at all the beautiful colors, like the rainbow with small strips of color turning slowly in a circle going up, with amazing light bouncing off the colors.

As I float I forgot all about the hard life of earth. The worry, the tiredness all gone. As I got to the top, I saw a figure of a man standing over me. His soothing voice said come see the wonders to come. Then his voice said time to go back. I begged to stay he answer no; it is not yet your time. Then he said I want you to know. I will be there when you need me.

He spoke again, saying what you have seen and hear, will not go back with you. Know I will be with you until.

No Honor

God has made us what we are; in our union with Christ Jesus he has created us for a life of good deeds, which he has already prepared for us to do. People minds are in the dark, there values are of the evil one. People have no honor for their parents or family. They have lost all feeling of shame. People do all sorts of indecent things without shame. People have deceitful desires with no meaning of life, for them self or others. God said love your neighbor as you love yourself. Do people today even know the Ten Commandments; this is a good place to start.

Your heart and minds must be made new. You must put yourself in Gods likeness. In a life that is upright and holy. Do not let your angry lead you into sin. Don't give the devil a chance. Do not use harmful words to your parents or anyone. Get rid of all bitterness and anger. Do not insult each other, hateful feelings belong to the evil one. Learn to forgive each other, as God has forgiven you through Jesus Christ.

Your life should be controlled by love. Do not let greed, sexual immorality or indecency control you. Watch your language no obscene, profane, or vulgar language to your parents or anyone. Do not let Gods anger come upon you. Stay in the light; do not go into the darkness. Live in the light of God. It is the light that brings a rich harvest. Try to learn what pleases our lord. Don't live like ignorant people, because these are evil days.

Put on all the armor that God gave you, so you will be able to stand-up against the devils evil tricks. We are not fighting against each other; we are fighting against the wicked forces of today. Carry your faith as a shield against the evil one. God wants us to honor our mother and father. Just think about it, God wants us to honor our parents. This shows how unselfish God is, Because God want you to honor him. And he also gave this respect to our parents. How great is God! In my day our parents put the fear of God in us. To make a point, we did not dear raise a hand to our parents. We did not dear open our mouth back to them. We would bite our tongues first. Even if we had to bite it off (smile).

No One Knows

The Bible tells us in (Matthew 24:36-37) that no one knows the time except the Father. Matthew 24: 37 say the coming of Jesus will be like what happened in the time of Noah. In the day of the flood people ate and drink, people got married, everyone went on with their daily life, not realizing what was happening until the flood came and swept them away.

The bible said this is how it will be when Jesus comes. Christ will come when you are not expecting him. That's why Jesus said watch always; this means when you see signs today that are given in the bible you know the time is near. That is good reason to read the word, so you can recognize the signs of Jesus return. Will you be ready for his return? Have you welcome the Lord into your life. Do you stay in the light with Jesus, or do you live in the dark.

You still have time to call on your Lord, he is waiting for you, and it is never too late. Repent your sins and go to the light of your Lord. Do not get lost in the dark, the path is easy and will burn out. The light is soothing and bright, and will last forever. So follow the narrow path into the light, take his hand he will lead you there. It's time to open your heart, repent and praise the Lord your God always.

In Luke 21: 20-22 Jesus gives a sign, when you see Jerusalem surrounded by armies, then you know that it will soon be destroyed. This will be "The Days of Punishment" to make true all that the Scriptures say. So watch the sky you will see strange things happening to the sun, the moon, and the stars. Then you will know you salvation is near.

But you should not worry; we should live with hope and love, because on this earth there is always danger. Our life on this earth is short and we could have a crisis at any moment, so don't worry about the last days. We just need to be aware at all times, because we could meet with death through an accident or illness, or by a deranged gunman. Do not worry about your life, just live and work in God's Spirit always.

Obey God

Always obey God obedience to God will bring you many blessings. Disobedience to God is the devil at work, this will bring you down and you will go to the dark. If you are uncertain about what God wants from you ask God to guide you. Ask God for deliverance from your sins. Never try to live without God, because the second chose is Satan, so please obey the Lord your God.

As I see generation come and go I pray for the people of earth today. People are losing, and have lost their spiritual morals, plus they have lost all morals if they ever had any. Generations of today don't seem to have any morals or respect. Without the law of morals God gave all people, this earth as we know it today will soon deteriorate into a ball of evil. I wish I could say this is not what my eye sees and my heart feels.

But I'm afraid I see things going in the wrong direction. Evil does not know day or night any time is good for evil deeds. There was a time when evil was done only in the dark. But now Satan is gaining strength, that's why evil no longer hide in the dark. The spirit of evil is building his army. God is calling his people to strength their faith and obedience, for his son Jesus Christ.

Jesus is your hope; help Jesus shine in the face of evil through your faith and prayer's. Let God know you are with him and you want to be his people. Let God know you will not turn from him. Truth, love, and peace are with the Lord your God. For lack of faith and disobedience brings corruption. Follow Jesus into the light of love for all God's people. Fear not for God is with you.

Our Human Nature

What our human nature wants, and what the spirit wants is opposed. Our human nature and our spirit are enemies. We fight with our self from within. Our human nature is quite plain, it is immoral and filthy, our human nature has indecent actions, it worship idols and witchcraft. People fight each other, they become jealous and angry at each other, and they are envious. People who are like this will not possess the Kingdom of God. Let God direct your lives, and you will not satisfy the desires of human nature.

The fruit of the Spirit produces love, joy, peace, patience, kindness, goodness, faithfulness, humility and self-control. If you belong to Jesus Christ your human nature must control its passions and desires. You must not be jealous and irritate one another. The Spirit never ever judge people. The spirit is kind and gentle and endures long suffering.

The human nature produces adultery, fornication, selfish ambitions, murders and more. True believers want to do the will of God. Anyone who obeys our Lords words is a wise man, who is building treasures in heaven. Do not let man be your judge or leader, you know what God wants. You will know the evil one by what he do and say. Do not judge others for God will judge you the same way you judge others. Remember the gate to hell is wide and the road that leads to it is easy.

The Lord tests his people from time to time, to see how they weather the storm. If your life is built on Jesus and his wisdom, you will weather the storm. But life built without Jesus will collapse. Stay obedience to Jesus and there is no storm you will not weather. Know that every test you pass, the more treasures you are building in heaven. Yes you will get your riches in heaven. Never ever put your whole faith on any human being. Put your faith in your King Jesus Christ.

People judge as if their way is the right way, when they know only their way. People think everyone should be like them and do what they do. God made people to be different, so they can learn from each other. They may know a better way or different way. But you will never know that way because your mind is closed to only your way. If God wanted us to be alike he would have made us alike. People that do not judge are wise people, because they can open their minds to the universe. If we seek the Kingdom of God, all our needs will be supplied.

Our Time Is Short

Wake-up our time is short. Matthew tells us people will change but not for the better. People will hate one another, they will betray each other. They will give up their faith. Plus as we get closer to the end, there will be many false prophets. There will be a wide spread of evil among people over the whole world. So keep your faith in Jesus so you don't burn, the fire is hot. Hate will flourish the closer we get to end times. Stay with the Lamb (Jesus) his light will lead the way.

People will hate you and persecute you because you love the Lord. Just hold strong you will be glad you did. Satan will come and preach his gospel all over the world. That's why you need to know Gods words so you can save yourself from the evil one, and live forever. You just stay in the light, and stay with Jesus.

In Luke 21: 20-24 the word talks about Jerusalem being surrounded by armies. This means Jerusalem desolation is near; when this happen the Lords clock is ticking faster end time is near. The word tells us these are the days of vengeance, the Lords vengeance. Wake-up time is short. Today people are still fighting with and about (Israel) Jerusalem. I do remember reading something like; you mess with Israel you mess with God! Jesus is coming to judge the world. When he comes he will dispatch his angels to gather his believers living and dead.

People

People have change they no longer look at you, there is no eye contact. It's as if, they were to make eye contact, you would see all their evil deeds. People friends are through the wire (cyber space) so they need not make eye contact. People have trade-up their families for friends. There friends are now their family. There was a time when they had both family and friends. They give and show love for friends and show hate and envy for family. People have thousands of cyber friends, people they do not know and have not seen. What's wrong with this picture, or is it me! Do you sometime feel you are in the wrong world, not the world from God?

When you go to the doctor do they look at you, do they make eye contact? Can they service you and never make eye contact? They seem to be trying very hard not to look at you. People do not want to know you, they just make judgments about you and believe whatever their mines tell them about you, and then they hate you.

We are at a time when family wants to see other family members do badly. They do not want their family to receive God's blessing. They think God's blessing is only for them, because of a certain thing they did. People use to pray for their family to be blessed by God. Now they curse their family members and pray for the worse, for their family.

People are hurting each other from hear say, from the word of one person. They do not look for the truth. They just spread the lie. From that lie they will do you in. Beware Satan's helpers are everywhere. Stay in the light and pray to God every day.

People Must

People must take responsibility for their own sin.
People must ask the Lord to forgive them of their sin.
People must change and renew their heart and spirit.
People must hope and pray for our nation under God.
People must have a need for peace and happiness.
People must praise and honor our God and Savior.
People must glorify our King Jesus.
Everything he does is right and just, and he can humble anyone who acts to proudly. Praise to the King.

I always wonder if there is some importance to the number seven, because our God seam to use that number a lot. What do you think?

God rested on the seventh day. The temple candlestick held seven candles. The Lord addressed seven churches. Revelation speaks of seven spirits, and then there are seven golden candlesticks, seven seals, seven trumpets, seven thunders, and seven vials. I'm sure there are lots more for the number seven.

Pray

As we go on with our life don't forget God. For God is the kingdom, the power and the glory forever and ever. Put the Lord in your life every day. Always pray in the name of Jesus. If you think you have nothing to pray about. You can always use the" Lord's Prayer" to honor our God, or use your own words in Jesus name. The Lord's Prayer goes something like this:

Our Father who are in heaven. Holy is your name. Your kingdom come. Your will be done, on earth as it is in heaven. Lord give us this day our daily bread. And forgive us our trespasses as we forgive those who trespass against us. And lead us not into temptation. But deliver us from evil. For God is the kingdom the power and the glory forever and ever. Amen

What is this prayer saying? Give us this day our daily bread is asking God to provide our daily meal. Forgive us our trespasses, as we forgive those who trespass against us. We are asking God to forgive us for our sins and we will forgive those who sin against us. Lead us not into temptation we are asking God to help us not do evil deeds. And deliver us from evil is asking God to keep us safe from the evil one.

Your kingdom come you are letting God know you believe in his kingdom and his son Jesus Christ.

Your will be done, we are letting God know we approve of him and love him by honoring his will, and letting him know his will is just.

Prayer before Starting Work

I was thinking about the working people. Then I remember a prayer someone send me. It is a prayer for work for your job. Some people have problems at work. Some co-workers like to make it hard for others. Even when you are giving your job the best you have. Just remember you are working for God first. If Satan is on the job with you, use this prayer to cast out that evil spirit, and have a great day at work. Then praise God for your Job. The Author of this prayer is unknown.

I know you will love it, I pray the Lords light will shine on you. My heavenly Father, as I enter this work place, I bring your presence with me. I speak your peace, your grace, your mercy, and your perfect order into this office. I acknowledge your power over all that will be spoken, thought, decided, and done within these walls. Lord, I thank you for the gifts you have blessed me with. I commit to using them responsibly in your honor.

Give me a fresh supply of strength to do my job. Anoint my projects, ideas, and energy; so that even my smallest accomplishment may bring you glory. Lord, when I am confused, guide me. When I am weary, energize me. When I am burned out, infuse me with the light of the Holy Spirit.

May the work that I do and the way I do it bring faith, joy, and a smile to all that I come in contact with today.

And oh Lord, when I leave this place, give me traveling mercy. Bless my family and home to be in order as I left it. Lord, I thank you for everything you've done, everything you're doing, and everything you're going to do. In the name of Jesus I pray, with much love and thanksgiving.

Aman

Punishment

When you don't honor and follow God's commands his punishment can be great. Read (Leviticus 26: 14-46). God said if you do not obey his commands and laws he will bring disaster on you. God will also bring incurable diseases and cause your life to waste away. Whenever you go against God, he will go against you. Anything you try to do will not turn out right, or will not happen for you.

God said he can make you so terrified you will think someone is after you when no one is chasing you, or doing anything to you, he can put this on your mind and keep you running. If you are still against God he will increase your punishment seven times, this could go on for years. I do know I would not want the Lord against me. Some people seem to always have things go wrong for them, sometimes it's just in their mind. They need to stop and bring the Lord into their heart and life.

Life is short so turn to the Lord your God, and ask him to come into your life. When the good Lord is against you all your hard work will do you no good. He can make your life very dark and dangerous. So come from the dark into the light of Jesus Christ. If you continue to defy the Lord he will continue to punish you and make your punishment harder and harder. So find the light, do not be afraid to step into the light of Jesus. He is waiting for you.

When you are not living with God he can cut off your food supply. And when you do get food and you have eaten it, God can still make you feel hungry, as if you eat nothing. I say to you stay in the light of the Lord your God, and let him provide for your needs. God wants to provide for you because he loves you and wants you to be his people. The Lord only wants your love and respect and in return he will give you so much more.

People know that you can make our Lord so angry that he may not accept your prays any more. Read (Leviticus 26: 27-32) in (Leviticus 26: 40-46) lets us know how good God is after his people rejected him over and over again, God still promise not to completely abandon or destroy them. When you are good to the Lord our God he is good to you. He can make it were you will not have to borrow from anyone. You will always prosper and never fail, if you are faithful to your Lord.

Praise and honor your God and remember do not go against him, because he can and will curse everything you do. Do not bring yourself under God's punishment the Lord your God is so great he can make trouble stay with you until you die (Deuteronomy 28). God can constantly oppressed and make you receive harsh treatment, your suffering can make you lose your mind. So I ask that you follow the light of Jesus Christ, so these things never come to you.

Pure Evil

The Antichrist always try to be like Jesus, but in evil form he tries to copy whatever Jesus did in an evil way. God loves his dwelling place Jerusalem, and God hates Babylon it was always filled with evil. When the Antichrist comes at end-time he will make Babylon now known as Baghdad his headquarters and dwell in this place where demons and all evil dwell (Revelation 18).

During this time people will push God away and dismiss him. People will turn to demonic spirits. People will believe in unclean spirits, there world and life will be very dark they will be worse off than when they believed in God. Read (Luke 11: 24-25), and (Jeremiah 51: 7). At end-time the new rebuilt Babylon will be known as the place to be. People will seek pleasures and activities that will be purely evil.

People will be unfaithful to God in every way possible. With the Antichrist as the head of Babylon, and as the head of the world, people can do no wrong every evil thing goes. In the last day's evil will be so profane the only way to stop it is, for God to destroy it all. When God judges the evil of the world it will be swift and final. Read (Revelation 18:5-7) and (Proverbs 16:18).

Pure evil will be no more, lift your heads for your Lord Jesus Christ is coming. After Jesus defeat the Antichrist, God will bring a New Jerusalem that will descend from heaven. The New Jerusalem will be the capital city of the new earth, and the eternal dwelling place of God and his people (Revelation 21). I say to you today make yourself one of God's people, stay in the light of Jesus.

Qualities

Do your best to add goodness to your faith.
To your goodness add knowledge
To your knowledge add self-control
To your self-control add endurance
To your endurance add godliness
To godliness add Christian affection
To your Christian affection add love
These are the qualities all Gods people
Should have.

Rapture

What is the Rapture? The Rapture is the time before the Tribulation period, the time before the Antichrist comes. We are now living in the Church Age. The Church Age started 50 years after Jesus Christ death. The Church Age does not have anything to do with a building as in a church, it is more of a protection that God has over the world to hold down most of the demons from the world for our sake.

The Rapture is the coming worldwide evacuation by God. There will be a day during this time when God will remove his people from the world, before the chaos and destruction to come. God will remove all his true Christians so they would not have to go through any of the world's chaos that is to come. This will bring panic to every household, city and country, because people they know will disappear right before their eyes never to be seen again.

There will be missing, relatives, missing kids, missing friends and others. God will give no warning people will just disappear. This will happen in every city and in every nation. Husband's wives will vanish. Wives husbands will disappear from their arms. People will be loss with grief, there will be confusion threw out the whole world. God will manifest all his true believers. Yes God is going to Rapture all his true Christians before the Tribulation period, before the Antichrist comes.

God's true believers will be spared the trauma to come. Please do not confuse the Rapture and the Second coming of Jesus Christ, these are two different events. The return of Jesus is coming after the Rapture; his coming is during the Tribulation period, close to the end of the Tribulation period. I say to you put your trust in your Lord Jesus don't miss the Rapture, stay in the light of Jesus.

Rapture My Love Ones

When God comes to Rapture his believers you may wonder, what will happen to your love one's who have already died. God's plan includes both the living and the dead in the Rapture. For God has only put the dead asleep. Your human body goes back to the earth, and your spirit goes to your Lord where it stays asleep until the Lord calls for you. Just as Jesus died and rose again, so will the Lord raise the spirit of your love ones.

For when you enter heaven you are given a new body a pure body. The believers that are alive will not precede the people who are asleep, for the dead will rise first. Then we who are alive shall be caught up to gather in the air, to meet the Lord in a cloud. You will see your love one's again, if they are a believer they will be summon at the Rapture. The entire Lord's true believers and their love ones will always be with the Lord.

The Lord keeps asleep all his believers until he calls the ones who sleep within him. As long as your love one died believing in Jesus, they too will have God's gift of eternal life. The Lord's call will only be heard by those who have placed their trust in Jesus Christ. Please read the following and stay in the lord's light.

Hebrews 11:5
2Kings 2:11
2Corinthians 12:2-4
1Corinthians 15:20-52
1Thessalonians 4:13-18
Acts 1:10-11

Resist

If a man is not thoroughly honest in his desire, to find out the truth in religion. If he privatcly cares for anything more than Gods praise, he will go on to the end of his days doubting, dissatisfied, and restless, and will never find the way to peace. Because he is dissatisfied, he will blame everyone and everything for his restlessness. In his doubt he will never blame himself. For he see himself as being right and perfect. In his restlessness he sees himself above everyone and even above God.

I think this is a form of being possessed by the evil one. When this person praise himself by telling his self he is perfect, he is also telling Satan he is perfect. Satan is feeding from him. It is this person responsibility to exercise his authority and resist the devil. Renounce participation in the evil ones schemes. Confess your sins unto the Lord your God, in the name of Jesus. And forgive those whom have offended you. Go to them that you have offended and give your love unto them and unto the Lord your God.

Go in through the narrow gate, because the gate to hell is wide and the road that leads to it is easy. There are many who travel it. Look for the gate to life, it is hard and there are few people who find it. Matthew 7: 13. Be on your guard against false prophets. They come to you like sheep on the outside. They are really like wild wolves on the inside. (Matthew 7: 15). Any tree that does not bear good fruit is cut down and is thrown into the fire. (Matthew 7: 18-19). You will know the false prophets by what they do and say.

Respect God

God do not want man to fear him. God wants us to have a holy respect for him.

That is what fear God means. Man does not respect each other, so how can they have respect for our God. We are all God's children. If we do not respect each other, how can we respect our father and brother Jesus? Jesus said "The Father judges no one" because God committed all judgments to the Son Jesus.

Jesus is in charge of the judgments and their timing. I once asked why he made the bible so hard to understand. Then I receive a holy answer. If he had made it easy for us, we would not seek out his word.

This means to study and seek out the Lords word. So we will know the true word. Not the words of man.

Not all men seek his words, they settle for the words of man. Seek and you shell find.

Ride with God

I sometimes think back on my child hood. I have realized that some things that I went through as a child helped me in my adult life. I realize that if I had not gone through some things, I would not have been able to cope with some things in my adult hood. My child hood gave me strength to deal with things in my life today. I realize that God was installing things in me that I could use later in life.

I believe our lives are somewhat planed in advance by God. It's like he gave us a push, and then let us make our own choses. You may make a right or wrong turn, but God put it out there for you to choose. After that some things happen because of the choses you made. If you stay right with God even if you make a wrong turn, he can change your directions, and make it better for you. Through my life I have made a wrong turn, and have felled the Lord change my direction, and made it right for me.

He can do the same for you. So never ever give up on our Lord. This is where you praise our Lord and give him thanks for everything he has done for you. So the next time when you are in the driver seat, God will ride along with you. This is why you need to keep the Lord in your life. Because there will be tomorrow.

Salvation

Your God would like to give you salvation. Do you want Salvation it can be accomplished through our Lord and Savior Jesus Christ? Salvation is God's revelation to humanity. Through Jesus, God wants to rescue us from danger, harm, and death. Our Lord Jesus can rescue you from your sins and from death. You must renew your spirit and call on Jesus to lead a life that is morally pleasing to God.

You need a relationship with God, because your sins will separate you from God. Life without God is like a bad hair day every day. Go to the light and restore your relationship with your Lord If you are a sinner you are separating yourself from your Lord. Look to Jesus for God's salvation, godlessness is from the dark. God is holy he will provide salvation for his people, God will not tolerate sin and will always save and redeem you, for he loves you so.

Repent to Jesus so the Father will offer you salvation. You can have life in the name of Jesus if you believe God's son is the Messiah. Through your faith in Jesus, God will give you salvation. You must repent and believe have faith and trust in Jesus, and God will give you eternal salvation. God promise you salvation, eternal life with Jesus (John 3:16) and (1John 2:25). Salvation is a gift from God so you and I can live on in Jesus Kingdom to come (Romans 3:21-26).

Shameful

Do not shame your Lord, your life must be controlled by love. God's people should not be involved in sexual immorality or indecency, or greed profane or vulgar language. I know a woman, when she spoke every other word that came out of her mouth was vulgar language. She had three kids; she spoke this way around her kids. When I look at her kids, I know what they would be like when they grow up; they will be speaking the same language or worst. Need more be said.

No one who is immoral, indecent, or greedy will receive a share in the Kingdom of Christ. Did you know greed is a form of idolatry? Because a person who is in love with money, worships money they do not worships God! You should give thanks to God. It is those things that make Gods anger come upon you. Obey the Lord and live in his light. If you are Gods people you belong in the light, the light will bring you a rich harvest in heaven. Have nothing to do with things that belong to the darkness. You will only burn in the dark.

Sign's

At the end of age evil will no longer be restrained. God will remove his Holy Spirit from the earth. Everyone should keep their eyes on Israel. Israel is the indicator, when you see the nation begin to come to life. The population of Israel will exceed. Making Israel the most densely populated developed country in the world. There will be a serious shortage of land for residential construction in Israel. Look to Israel, the end is soon approaching. The sign of Jesus coming will appear in the sky.

Keep watching, our Lord Jesus will shine like the sun in all his brilliance. He will be so bright all the nations of earth will see him. Nations will hate Israel. Earth quakes and storms will get worse and worse. There will be an increase in wars and diseases. When you see or hear all these things happening at the same time, you will know it is close not far away. While all this is going on and then there's the Antichrist coming in the form of a man.

He will be voted in office and loved by most all men. The Antichrist will bring false peace treaties to Israel. He will then bring a one world religion that will be approved by the government. Wide spread sin will drive many from God. There will be a collapse of social order without God. The Antichrist will declare that he is God. Natural disasters will be great, like none you have ever seen. Keep your eyes on Israel.

People much wake-up the stage is being set, for the Antichrist to force himself on the world. Religious ignorance is one of Satan's favorite tools. Watch out for one world government that brings one world religion. Jesus said watch out that no one deceives you. (Matthew 24:4).If people refuse the Antichrist it will be dangerous he will have you killed. He will deny you food, water, medicine, and electricity. It will be illegal to refuse the Mark of the Beast.

People will betray their parents, brothers, sisters, and friends, for food and water. Read: Genesis 12:3 and Matthew 24:6.

Sinners

Luke 16: 19-25 tells us when sinners die, they are buried and there sole's go to hell, where they are in great pain from fire. When the Lords good servants die, there soles are carried away by angels to a holding place at the feast in heaven with Abraham, where they enjoy themselves waiting to see God. Jesus knows people are bound to sin, but do not make sin happen.

So watch what you do and say (Luke17: 1-4). Jesus died for us so the Father would forgive our sins, if we repent unto the son Jesus Christ. So always pray and repent your sins be very careful not to play with the almighty God, because he knows your heart. Do you think you can do the same sin over and over, and repent for the same old sin forever? Beware God is no fool!

Do not be a slave to money. You cannot serve both God and money. The things that are considered of great value in man's sight are worth nothing in Gods sight. Not everyone who think they know the password to heaven will have access to heaven, sorry. Jesus is the resurrection and the life. Those who believe in Jesus shall never die. For Jesus is the source of life, he has the power to give life and raise the dead. So put your life in Jesus hands depend on him, for he is life.

Eternal life is for people who trust and put their destiny in Jesus.

Stay Ready

Christian should stay ready for Christ return. You would think people would take care to live as God would have them live. You should stay ready knowing that our Lord and Savior, Jesus is coming. But fallen humans do not always have common sense. We should be living as if Jesus is coming at any moment. He could be here tomorrow or this weekend. Just stay ready for his return.

God has giving the warnings loud and clear; we receive warning every day, with all the signs pointing to the end to come. But people chose to ignore the signs. I pray you still have time to put your name in the Book of the Lamb, so you will hear Jesus trumpet when he calls his people to meet him in the clouds to enter heaven. Jesus will evacuate all his true believer's from the earth, and redeem them from this lawless world. Jesus will deliver his people from the wrath to come.

People, who do not have a genuine relationship with Christ, will be caught up in the day of trial, which shall come upon the whole world. Our Lord Jesus will keep his believer's from the day of trial. Jesus will give his people salvation, because he promised that believer's will not experience the horrors that will come upon the world. If your name is not in Jesus "Book of Life" Jesus said no flesh would be saved.

When all believers are removed from earth, the Spirit of God will be removed from the world also, and there will be no light, and anyone who still dwells on earth will not be saved. In heaven we shall be children of God, and we shall be like him, and we shall see him as he is. Under God's roof we shall be purified, as he is pure. I tell you now turn to the light; the light is Jesus before it is too late.

Go now to the light so you will hear Jesus call, for only the righteous will hear. Will you be left behind to experience the horrors that will be worse than anything the world has seen? Do not wait call on him, for the Lord waits for you. Please read your Lord's words.

1Thessalonians 5:9, 1Thessalonians 1:10, 1Thessalonians 4:17-18
Matthew 5:13-14, Matthew24:21-22
Revelation 3:10, Revelation 21:27
Titus 2:11-14
Philippians 3:20
2Peter 3:11
1John 3:2-3

Strong Faith

Have you read the book of Daniel from the Old Testament? You can feel the faith that Daniel and his friends had in God. Their faith was so strong I could feel it coming through the pages. I believe some of their faith jump into me, and God gave me this urgency to write and tell you about your Lord Jesus Christ. Daniel risked his life for his believe in God, and God did not let Daniel down, he blessed him for having so much faith in him.

Daniel and his friends refused to worship the king's idol. So the king threatened to burn them alive. Daniel told the king, our God we save us from the burning furnace. Daniel prayed and talked to God every day because he would not default his God, because of his faithfulness. So the king had Daniel thrown into the lion's den, but the lion's did not touch Daniel, because God send angles to protect him.

This tells us if our faith is strong our Father will be there for us. So let your faith stand your ground, and put your heart into your faith. God saved Daniel and his friends from the evil king again and again, and your God will be there for you like he was for Daniel and his friends. Read Lamentations 3:21-26 the Lord is my portion; says my soul, therefore I hope in him.

It is good that one should hope and wait quietly. For God is the God of hope (Romans 15:13). Read (Isaiah 40:3) those who hope in the Lord shall renew their strength and mount up with wings like eagles.

Supreme Ruler

God is our supreme ruler over all people and all nations. God will always win, and his will be done. God is holy and he does not lie, for he is just. God has authority over all things, and we should recognize him as our Lord and God in heaven who is holy. Our Lord God fills the universe with his glory, so we may find peace in his son Jesus Christ. God loves you as his own, for he is your Father.

No matter how much evil that's in man's heart God is willing to forgive your sin, by repenting unto his son Jesus. He does this because he loves you so and wants you to love him back. God knows our hearts are sinful by nature, sin that we inherited from Adam and Eve. We are under the presence of God's Spirit so that our selfish sinful ways do not bring destruction upon our self.

God's good grace protects us from our self. God gives everyone a change to be his people he waits for you. God will give you salvation he pours his Spirit on all who believe and call on his son. So let go of your evil ways and be transformed by God's love. Have Faith in our Lord Jesus and trust in him for he is for you. Build your endurance, for Satan will surely try to make you fall. So you much shine before our Lord and trust in him.

Swollen with Pride

How different things are today we see in the news and with our nations signs and shadows of coming events predicted and prophecy that give feeling and sight of the end time approaching. This in itself should make us live a more committed life too our savior Jesus Christ. In the last days (2 Timothy 3:1-5) say people will be headstrong and treacherous and swollen with pride.

It says people will be selfish, greedy, boastful and conceited; they will be insulting, disobedient to their parents, ungrateful and violent. They will be unkind, merciless, slanderers, and reckless, they will have no love for each other. All this is a sign of end times. (2 Timothy 3:6) tell us to keep away from such people. Everyone who wants to live a godly life in union with Jesus Christ will be persecuted by others 2Timothy3:12. I think people with demon sprits can sense the present of the Lord in a godly person.

That's why you need to stay in the Holy Scriptures, which is able to give you the wisdom that leads to salvation through faith in Jesus Christ. 2Timothy 3: 16-17 says all scripture is inspired by God and is useful for teaching the truth, rebuking error, correcting faults, and giving instruction for living right. So that the person who serves God may be fully qualified and equipped to do every kind of good deed in Jesus name.

Wake up it's time to clean your souls. Just open your eye and ears; we are slowly preparing the way for the Antichrist. You can see and hear the disobedient in our children of today. Our children are conceited and ungrateful they are selfish and insulting. As time past this will get worse, because they will past it down to their kids. People it's time to change your evil ways. Stay in the light and go to Jesus he is your friend always.

The Dark Side

The coming of the Antichrist or the lawless one will be in accordance with the work of Satan. Displayed in all counterfeit miracles, signs and wonders, and in every sort of evil that deceives those who are killed. They perish because they refused to learn the truth and be saved. God will judge them for rejecting the truth about his son, and for enjoying their life of sin. Multitudes will perish because they will not listen to the "Word of God".

The Antichrist will tell people he is God. Rebellion against God will increase. The love of many will turn cold. They will follow other religions. They will be in touch with evil spirits. They will listen to the man of sin. Satan the man of sin, so open your minds and know when to walk away. The demons will be liars, religious pretenders, false preachers, and counterfeit Christians.

There will be an increase in wickedness people will hate and betraying each other. Children will rebel against their parents, and have them put to death. There will be no love in the world. The Antichrist and his followers will slander the name of God. People will be without self-control. People will be brutal and they will kill and behead each other.

The Antichrist will be against all good things of God. He will do anything to break the "Ten Commandments". So pray always for our children and the future of our nation, in the name of Jesus (Isaiah 54:4). A day is coming when human pride will be ended and human arrogance destroyed.

The Date

Someone ask me why I don't date my work. I could not give an answer. I just know I did not want to date them. Later a holy answer came to me. Saying the little things is not always important. Then my answer came. There is no date it is for tomorrow, it is for today, it is for yesterday. It is forever. It is for the end of time. Today, tomorrow and yesterday. For God is forever and always. There is no date tomorrow or yesterday, today is today. God is yesterday, tomorrow, and today. For Gods date is forever and ever. That is the date.

The Day When

The day when the Lord will sit in judgment is near. The day of the Lord is a day of darkness. The clock is ticking. The end of time as we know it is fast approaching. The signs are everywhere. Watch and listen. He will stand on the "Mount of Olives" to the East of Jerusalem. The Lord our God will come bringing all the angels to carry out his will. When this will be is known only to the Lord. Watch and listen. You will hear the noise of battles and war close by.

And the news of battles and war far away Matthew 24:3. There will be many false prophets to fool many people. Many will give up their faith. There will be a wide spread of evil, as you have never seen. This evil will be worldwide. People's heart will grow cold. They will betray one another, and hate one another. Keep Jesus in your heart and you will be saved. Pray now pray always in the name of Jesus.

The Expressions of God

The Father, the Son, and the Holy Spirit. These are three different expressions of God. Jesus is in the Father and the Father is in Jesus. They to gather are the Holy Spirit, they are one. Jesus was not a man who became God. Jesus is God who became a man. Jesus is the expression of God in human form. Know Jesus and you know God. The word of God is an extension of God himself. The word of God has a name Jesus and a title Christ.

There is and always will be only one God. God's expression of himself is in Jesus Christ. God is one, the Father, the Son, and the Holy Spirit. The Blessed Trinity one being in three personalities. Jesus Christ is God's living word. Man should live by every word that proceeds from the mouth of God. (Matthew 4:4).

The First Fruit

The first fruit of the Holy Spirit is love. For love is of God. For God created the world. Then God created you to live in his world. God loved the world he created. And God loved the people he created to live in his world. God would like you his people to return that love to each other and to the world he created. God would like to know that you can love more then you hate.

Eat of the first fruit, the fruit of love. As God looks upon the creation he loves. His first fruit has rotten and fallen to the ground. Worms has put holes in his fruit of love. His Holy Spirit is waiting to feel the warmth of your love, so he can plant more love for his people. As he shares his fruit of love with his people the sun shine's bright and all is right.

The Last Days

In (2 Timothy 3:1-5) tells us the last days will be difficult times. People will be selfish, greedy, boastful, and conceited; they we be insulting, disobedient to their parents, ungrateful, unkind, merciless, slanderers, violent and fierce. They will also hate good people.

When I read this I said to myself, people are like that today. So are we in the last days now? What do you think? I would answer this question with a no not yet. I think we are getting close. People will be a lot worse in the last days; we have not seen anything yet.

God prophecy said the Rapture will come before the last days. The Rapture will be when Jesus calls all his believers to meet him in the clouds. People will be Rapture from all over the world. Jesus will just remove people from the earth, they will just disappear.

Our Lord will remove his people so they do not go through the Tribulation. How good is, our Lord and savior? That's why I say to all stay in the light with Jesus.

The Light of the World

Jesus is the light of the world, he is forgiveness. Jesus is a friend to sinners; he is a friend to everyone. Jesus is worthy and good, look to him for forgiveness; you will accomplish much with Jesus in your life. He will be honest and true to you. He will get you through your crisis. With the Lord by your side you are not helpless. Nothing is too difficult for the Lord, just have faith and he will be right at your side.

Do not believe lies and gospel about any one, seek out the truth. People have been killed over lies. Do not plan evil against each other, you know right from wrong. Evil acts will send you to the dark. Stay in the light. Our Lord will hold your hand through difficult, painful situation, you are not alone. Do not make assumptions about anything or anyone; take it to the Father through your brother Jesus Christ.

And know he is there for you. When life is hard call on Jesus and be respectful to everyone. Even the ones that do not deserve to be respected. They too will have to face almighty God. Stay in control for your reward will be great. The light will shine bright.

The Living Bread

Jesus is the living bread; he provides spiritual sustenance for a life giving relationship with God. You must go through Jesus to find eternal life. For Gods Spirit gives life through his son Jesus Christ. Whatever you do for your fellow man, you are doing for Jesus (Matthew 25:39-46). When you refuse to help your fellow man, you refuse to help Jesus; you then will go to eternal punishment in the lake of fire. All of Jesus righteous will have eternal life.

Jesus gave us a clock to keep time in Luke 21: 20-24 Jesus tells us about Jerusalem being surrounded by armies there will be armies from all nations, they will destroy Jerusalem. Jesus said this will be "The Day of Punishment". God's punishment will fall on all people. Luke 21: 25-28 his words say people will faint from fear as they wait for what is coming over the whole earth, your salvation is near very near.

I pray you find Jesus and stay in his light, for the Son of Man is coming. God ask that you believe in his son Jesus Christ. I do how about you, or do you like the dark where the evil one lives. God has giving you a chose so pick your destiny. When Jesus comes he will separate the righteous from the unrighteous Matthew 25:31-36. I say to you read The Word, so you will know the different between Gods

Word and man's word, the different between Jesus Words and Satan's word.

You will pick your own destiny by the things you do and say in this life. Our Father does not force anything on you the choice is yours. Jesus asks that you love one another as he have loved you. You must know that the source of temptation comes from Satan. You must strengthen your faith so Satan cannot touch you. Always keep Jesus in your heart. Jesus said he is the way, the truth, and the life and no one goes to the Father except through Jesus, because Jesus is the bread of life.

The Movie 2012

This was my second time watching the movie 2012. I could not help but think, the end of time could be like the movie. Then I thought how blessed we are. Next I thought we are fast approaching it. Open your eyes and ears. The good Lord is giving us many signs. If you watch the world news, then you know he is going around the world, from place to place trying to get our attention. See how the weather is changing. The government and people are broke. It's a global thing.

If your ears are open you know the word global is use a lot within government, it's a government word, and not a very good word beware. There's is nothing you and I can do about it. Whatever the government sends our way, we just have to deal with it. That is why you and I need Jesus with us. Today's people love evil. People become enemies they fight, they become jealous, angry, ambitious hurting and harming each other.

They form groups to criticize and joke about a person. Just to please the evil one they hold within. This is not good, mine your ways. For God is love, God is light. Luke 6:22-25, John 15:19. Blessed are you when men hate you, and exclude you, abuse you, and cast out your name as evil for man's sake. Rejoice in that day and leap for joy. For indeed your reward is great in heaven.

Christ came in order that we are put right with God through faith. It is through faith that all of us are Gods children in union with Jesus Christ, (Galatians 3:4). We were baptized into union with Jesus.

Therefore there is no difference between slaves and free people, between rich and poor, between men and woman, between your skin color and my skin color. We are all one in union with Jesus Christ.

Do you belong to Jesus? Then you are a descendant of Abraham and will receive Gods promise. As he promise Abraham. God sent the Spirit of his Son into our hearts. So cry out to your Father, for you are his child. You began by Gods Spirit; do you now want to finish by your own power? Why do you want to turn to those weak and evil ruling spirits, not of God why? Let love make you serve one another, as you serve our Lord. So we all can serve our Father as one union.

When the new world comes, I would like to be there, and I would like to see you all there. Jesus said my Father has many mansions, and I will prepare a place for you. Jesus asks his followers, have I became your enemy because I tell you the truth? Answer this question for Jesus and for yourself. May he shine his light on you. (Psalms 5: 2, 4, 11,) Give heed to the voice of my cry, my king, my God, who takes pleasure in wickedness, nor shall evil dwell with you. Let all those rejoice who put their trust in you.

Let them forever shout for joy, because you defend them, Matthew 5:38. Do not take revenge on someone who wrongs you. If someone slaps your right check, let them slap the left cheek too, Galatians 6. If you think you are something when you really are nothing, you are deceiving yourself. Do not deceive yourself; no one makes a fool of God. You will reap exactly what you plant.

If you plant in the field of your natural desires, from it you will gather the harvest of death. If you plant in the field of the Spirit, from the spirit you will gather the harvest of eternal life.

The New Holy City

The new holy city, the new world will be the new location of our Lord Jesus Christ. It will be the throne to King Jesus. All who overcome the evil of man and keep the faith will be praising and serving our God in the new city. The Father, Son and the Holy Spirit will be present to meet all our needs. The new city will have streets of pure gold. It will have mansions of gold and precious stones.

A river of crystal clear water and trees with twelve fruit will line the streets. Believers will eat and drink in the Holy City. There will be no more curses in the new creation. No pain, no sickness. As residents of the Holy City we will see the face of our Father. Believers will have the privilege to live forever (John 14:39). Jesus said there are many rooms in my Father's house, and I will prepare a place for you (John 14:6).

Jesus said I am the way, the truth and the life. No one goes to the Father except by me. Jesus is the bread of life. God raised the Lord Jesus to life; he will also raise us up into his presence. We are often troubled by things of this world. There are many enemies who come to destroy our faith. They give us doubt. Many time's we are badly hurt over and over again.

Do not despair; do not let them crush your faith. We always have a friend in Jesus. Keep your spiritual faith your blessing will be great. For what can be seen in this world will not last. What we cannot see will last forever. God has a home in heaven for us that will last forever. All of us must appear before Jesus to be judged. We will receive what we deserve according to everything we have said and done, good and bad.

So do not give up your new home to live in a fire pit. Your new home will be worry free. Anyone who is joined to Jesus Christ will have a new home with a new better life. Ephesians 1 if you believe in Christ, God will put his stamp of owner ship on you, by giving you the Holy Spirit. So stay in the light with Jesus and in joy your new worry free home.

The Seals

First seal: The white horse, the rider held a bow and was given a crown.
He rode out as a conqueror to conquer.

Second seal: The red horse, its rider was given the power to bring war on the earth.
He was given a large sword, so people will kill each other.

Third seal: The black horse, its rider held a pair of scales in his hand. The scales mean
People on earth will not have enough money to buy food.

Fourth seal: The pale-colored horse, its rider was named Death and torment (Hades).
This rider had authority over one fourth of the earth. Authority to kill by means of war, famine, disease, and wild animals.

Fifth seal: This seal hold the souls who were killed because they were faithful and proclaimed God's word. They asked Jesus to judge the people on earth soon. But Jesus told them to wait a little longer. He would not judge them just now.

Sixth seal: This seal holds a violent earthquake, and the sun will became black, and the moon will turn red like blood. Then the stars will fall to earth, and the sky will disappear, and every mountain and island will move from its place.

I did not write about the Seventh Seal, I will leave that for you, plus there is another small scroll for
Jesus to open, you should read Revelation 5, 6, 7, and 8.
Jesus said do not let these things scare you.
For if you live in the light of Jesus, you are under his protection.

The Ten Commandments

Exodus 20: 1-17
Do not murder
Do not steal
Do not bear false witness
Do love your neighbor
Do not use the Lords name in vain
Do not commit adultery
Do not desire another man's things
Honor your father and your mother
Worship no other God
Keep the Sabbath Holy

Luke 12: 7 Even the hairs of your head have all been counted.

Mark 3: 29 Whoever says evil things against the Holy Spirit will never be forgiven, because he has committed an eternal sin.

Mark 10: 27 With God all things are possible.

The Tribulation Begins

When the Lord Jesus Christ read Gods scroll he tells us about the events that will happen on earth during the early Tribulation period.

First Seal is a rider on a white horse this is the coming of the Antichrist.

Second Seal is a rider on a red horse this is bloodshed and war.

Third Seal is a rider on a black horse this is worldwide famine this is the world's sorrows.

With this famine will come much sorrow, Matthew 24: 7-8 tells us nations will rise against nations. Kingdom against Kingdom. This is the beginning of the world's sorrows. For the red horse and the black horse will ride side by side with much bloodshed and war. And it will be very hard for people to get food, and there will be many people dying by earthquakes.

During this time people will severely struggle to get by. The wealthy will have all they need, hardship will not touch them, and masses of poor people will not survive. In the world today we are seeing some change between the wealthy and the poor. Poverty is getting larger as we lose our jobs and homes, and the wealthy is getting richer. The wealthy is offering less and less help for the poor.

Man has become greedy and selfish. Today is like Robin Hood in reverse; the rich take from the poor, and give to the rich. As the rich become richer and the poor become poorer. And we are not even in the Tribulation period. So you can just see how bad it will be at that time. Today we are all facing the same struggles, some of us have been rich and now they are poor.

The middle class is slowly disappearing; you will be either poor or rich. And with each economic famine that comes the impact will be greater than the last. Your middle class neighbor will try to portend that it is not affecting them, but know if it affects you it affects your neighbor. Now is the time to stand too gather, because it is hard for everyone to live with less.

Above all stay in the light with Jesus, and do not worry what others think because it only matters what Jesus thinks of you. Because Jesus loves you and you love him back, he will have your back, trust and believe in your Lord Jesus Christ.

The Word of God

The word of God has a name, Jesus. The word of God has a title, Christ.

Jesus is the expression of God in human form. To know Jesus is to know God.

There is and always has been and will be only one God.

Gods expressing of himself in Jesus Christ does not change that.

There is one God in three expressions.

The Father, the Son, and the Holy Spirit.

Believe in his name means to adhere to, trust in, and rely on.

Jesus Christ is Gods living word.

Read:

John 1: 14-18
John 1: 10-13
John1: 1-2
John 1: 50-51

The World Hate's

Have you notice how people hate on each other. Have you notice how families hate on each other. I've seen people with no problems, but they make problems for them self, because all they have in their heart is hate. Father's hate their son's, but loves their daughter's. Mother's love their son's and hate their daughter's. There are all kinds of crazy hate in this world. The haters are in the dark.

I have even seen people get mad at one of their friends, and then turn and hate their other friends, because of what this one friend did. Hate is everywhere, they hate just because, and they hate to make them self-feel good. This is the only way some people know how to enjoy them self. You wouldn't believe how many ways there are for people to hate. Hate is their way of hiding their deep imbedded hurt.

There dark spirit wants others to feel what they feel. So they try to hurt others. People meet people and become friends. Then they tell their new friend, I do not like your friend, if you want to be my friend you can't be friends with that person. Believe it or not, this friend will break off a twenty year friend ship, to have a new friend they ready don't know much about.

There are young adults married with their own husband and children. And when their parents part, and choose a different partner. There grown children cannot live with that. They even have their own family. But will pick and pick, spending years trying break this relationship. If your parent is happy grow-up and let it be. Praise God for your husband and children, you now have your adult life. Why are you still acting like a baby? All those things will send you to the dark. They are all sins under God.

The Father wants you to love each other, not hate. God said love, and you do hate! Do you readily like fire? People no longer have compassion for the human race. This is your race; you are human, are you? You are killing each other. It's like you are hunting each other down like animals. My lord will they ever change? If not we are fast approaching the end of our time as we know it.

People say they love life, but by my eye's, we are like ants running around under the Lords foot, not knowing which way to go. I pray that Gods Words will bring us to the light. As Jesus light shine so bright, waiting for us to come. If only they would replace the hate with God's love for them. I pray for the hater's. I pray for us all. I pray our Lord have mercy on us.

There Is One

There is only one true God and if you fail to stand with God, then you are standing with Satan. I'm sorry but there is no in between. It's like yes or no, or day and night. There is the light and there is the dark. There is the good and there is the bad. There is the wicked and there is the blessed. There is God and no other, God is forever. God is today, tomorrow, yesterday, and always.

Jesus is the King, Jesus is salvation, God is the creator, God is the Father, and God is Jesus. And Jesus is God. God is the Holy Spirit, Jesus is the savior, and Jesus is the truth. God is The Word. God is life, God is glory. And God is the healer. There is one God and no other.

They Mourned for Him

Do you ever think that maybe we are all paying for Jesus death? When Jesus was nail to the cross he heard women mourn for him. Jesus said to them, do not weep for me, but weep for yourselves and for your children (Luke 23: 27-28). In this world we are all paying for the death of Jesus, that why we go through ups and downs in our life. Because we are all sinners and come up short of God's glory.

If God poured his wrath on his son to save us from our sin. What do you think you have coming, when he pours his wrath on the world. God offered his love we rejected it. Then he offered his son, and we rejected his son. Beware people the time is coming, not long not long. When Jesus was on the cross dieing they offered Jesus some wine with myrrh to ease his pain. But Jesus refused he was willing to take all the pain to save our souls (Mark 15: 23) (Luke 23:34) how great he is!

People do evil all day, every day then go to church on Sunday. As soon as they get out of church, they go back to their evil deeds. They think because they go to church and give an offering, they think they are saved but the Lord knows there heart. Let me tell you, you should rethink. Maybe you will get it the second time. Then again maybe not, maybe they love the dark. I do feel for them.

Let me tell you I am looking forward to my new, worry free home. I love the light; the light is all right with me. When Jesus died on the cross for our sins, he granted us the right to live with God in the new world. Plus he granted us eternity to live forever with God. Paradise, sweet paradise.

To Proud

Centuries have past the Lords Word has been heard and read over and over. Yet it has not saddle so man must suffer much and be rejected by people of today. Everyone living their life no one hears, no one see. Days go on people selling, planting, and building as if every day is promise to them. Jesus will come like a thief, some will be saved, and some will not, some will run, some will hide. Some will fear some will not. What will you do? What can you do?

For this is the coming of the Lord, are you too late, or are you ready. Will you ever be ready or not. Some of us think we are right with God when we are not. Some pray and tell God they are honest and right, and they are not like other people, so I thank you God I am not like them. Some of us repent and say forgive me God I am a sinner, please have pity on me, please let me be right with you Lord. Do you humble yourself unto God, or are you to proud?

Luke 21: 20-24 say when you see Jerusalem surrounded by armies, this will be "The Days of Punishment", to make come true all that the Scriptures say. On earth whole counties will be in despair (Luke 21: 20-24). People will faint from fear as they wait for what is coming over the whole earth. The Son of Man (Jesus) will appear, coming in a cloud with great power and glory. When these things begin to happen, your salvation is near.

That day will catch you like a trap. It will come upon all people everywhere on earth. Luke 19: 41 tell us Jerusalem was completely destroyed, because the people did not recognize the time when God came to save them. My question is will you recognize the time to call Jesus into your life, the time to ask Jesus to save you. He is your salvation in this life and in the new world to come. Stand firm believe and trust in the Lord your God.

To You My Lord

As I read the "Book of Revelation" The Smart Guide to the Bible Series, By Daymond R. Duck and Larry Richards. I just finish the last word of the last chapter. I got up took two steps forward and stopped. The Holy Spirit *came over me. I took two steps back and seat back down. I picked up my writing pad and pen from the table next to the chair; I just started writing I could not stop. It was God guiding my hand. He wanted me to write this and share it with everyone.*

I give myself to my savior Jesus Christ who I have served to the best of my ability. I promise to serve you my Lord for all times. Let it be your will, I shell honor and obey your will. Let it be written in our Father's house. I give myself to your only son, who gave his life for me, so I could walk in the house of my Lord. Jesus you are the Alpha and the Omega, the beginning and the end. For you are God.

The creator of all things, you are forever, the first and the last. Jesus you are the light of my world. Your glory is brighter than the noonday sun. There were none before you and there will be none after. There never was a time you were not there. Lord you will always be there because, you will always exist. I look upon your eyes Lord; they were every ware, beholding the good and the evil. I weep for them for they do not know God's glory.

For you my Lord, I stood firm against deception in the name of Jesus. I give you my love, my soul, my all. If in your eyes I have fallen, I do repent my sins unto you my savior Jesus Christ. I repent for breaking God's rules; I repent for knowing good but not doing good. I repent for all unrighteousness and all wickedness. I repent for ignoring God. For sin is a disease of the soul, the inner part of man. In the name of Jesus I repent. Lord let me eat from the tree of life, with you my Lord. For you are my first love.

Tragedy

Have you notice all the tragedy our nation has had. Does it make you think what is going on? And when our nation has these tragedies, why are they so destructive. Then I wonder could God be mad at our nation. Times are just bad with weather tragedies, high food prices, high fuel prices, we are losing our homes, our job, and I could go on. Is America becoming poor? The United States was once blessed by God, because we protected Israel.

Until America forced Israel into the Oslo Agreement, the land for peace formula. This formula called for Israel to give up some of the promise land in exchange for peace. Sounds like black mail to me. Then they divided Jerusalem and took part of that from the Jews. This land was promise to the Jews by God. In Genesis 12:3 God said anyone who have curse Israel, he would curse them. In Genesis 12:7 God told Abraham that he is giving the land of Canaan to him and his descendants.

In Genesis 15:18 God told Abraham I promise to give your descendants the land from the border of Egypt to the Euphrates River. In Genesis 17:8 God told Abraham the whole land of Canaan will belong to your descendants forever. Genesis 23:17 Tells how Abraham paid for the land of Canaan. Yes I do think God is very mad at the United

States about the promise land he gave to Abraham and his descendants. In Ezekiel 48: God divide some of the land among the tribes.

The Jews may not get their promise land until the Millennium, because man keeps short changing them. But God will keep his promise to Abraham no matter what! The Millennium is the return of Jesus Christ. There will be a new Kingdom on earth and Jesus Christ will be Lord and King to the whole earth. Some do not take God sincerely, the words come out of their mouth, but they are just learned words. Words with no meaning, not words from the heart.

So they test God and think they can do better than God, they test God out of selfish ambition. Let them without fault throw the first stone. You may ask why some nations oppressed Israel throughout history. I do not know the answer to this, but I think the nations do not believe in Jesus, because Israel does have enemies such as Egypt, North Korea, Russia, Germany, Rome and others.

God has put a heavy judgment on Israel's oppressors throughout history. So in my opinion I say yes, I do think God is mad at the United States for taking some of that land. I also think the tragedies and destruction will keep coming. I wonder what you would do about this!

Trust

God ask that you believe in his Son Jesus Christ. This means to trust Jesus, if you believe in him you will trust him. If you trust Jesus you will not worry about where your food and clothes will come from, God knows your needs read Luke: 12: 22-28. If you worry about your needs then there is no trust. The Lord can feel each and every one of us. So if your heart and soul is not open to Jesus you must worry, because God do not feel your spirit.

Your Lord Jesus will see to your needs, but not your wants. But if you believe and trust in him, your Lord will bless you so your wants will be gifts from God. And he will shower you with gifts just for making a place in your heart for him. In Luke 12:29-31 Jesus said don't be concerned about what you will eat and drink. Your Father God knows you need these things.

Jesus said instead, be concerned about his Kingdom. Trust in him and stay in the light, and wait for your Lord with a happy heart.

Under Our Nose

Islamic culture is growing in own country, but these are the people that hate Americans; the Muslim religion Islam is the fastest growing religion in America today. United States is under threat of global terrorism by Islamic culture. Americans do not take the threat of Islam seriously. The American people are too trusting, Islam people do not hide the fact that they hate Americans and want revenge.

Americans do not know what the revenge thing is about, at least I don't. But we invite them to live in our country. We Americans have no idea what they could be planning right under our nose. But as always the United States will be surprised when they stab us in the back, because we were so friendly and open to them. Do we know the true nature of this enemy? They could be all over our country planning and setting up for the big one.

The way I see it, if they hate us so much why are they living in our country among us, right under our nose. Why do we kept our backs turn towards the enemy? But listen people don't take me seriously; this is just what I think. What do I know I just needed to air out, before I get stale! I may not even know what I'm talking about, so close your ears you did not hear this, and I did not say this. The name Islam means submission.

Which means a Muslim is one who submits to God. So if there is any truth in the name Islam, the people much be great people. So do not agree with my words always seek out the truth so you will know the truth. I guess what I want to say is just beware always beware. Never ever harm anyone because of someone's words without knowing the truth. Because God loves all people, he even loves you. So always, did I say always stay in the light.

Wake Up

I say to you people wake up! Why do you sleep, you are not asleep in Jesus, cause you sleep in Satan. You let him pull your string like a puppet; he controls you when you don't let your parents control you. I say wake up, wake up people. Open your eyes and see the hold he has on you.

I say wake up and praise him who comes to free you. For the evil one will pull the string and trap you, and there is no return. I say to you people wake up, follow the light and sleep in Jesus. For the one who comes will wake you forever, and all will be well. So stay in the light with Jesus.

Walk

You must craw before you walk. If you walk with the Lord, he will take you all the way.

Walk with your head up right pass Satan. With the Lord by your side no one can touch you.

Satan will run to catch you, over and over again. You just keep walking with the Lord and

Satan will fall every time. If you complain you remain. If you praise, you will be raised.

Without the grace of God, we would perish.

Without the peace of God, we would be unsure of our salvation.

The source of grace and peace is the eternal God.

The God who is, who was, and who is to come.

The God who will always be.

War

There's a war coming that will top all wars. This war will be like none ever seen. This war will be at the end of the Tribulation Period. This war will be against Israel the smallest nation on earth. Satan will have six other nations against Israel, because Satan is against everything related to God. Satan will call other nations to meet him on Israel mountain top.

There will be six large nations plus a few others against Israel. Israel is only nine miles long, but they want to wipe Israel out. You may wonder why these nations are against Israel. These are God's people and God takes care of his people very well. Israel is a very wealthy nation for its size, Israel is wealthier then all the nations, and they do not like that fact. There are a number of nations today that hate Israel.

These nations wants to take Israel's land and wealth for them self. I would guest some of these nation are country's like Russia, Iran, Iraq, Ethiopia, and others, please read chapter's thirty eight and thirty nine of Ezekiel. Listen do not worry God will protect his people, they will not be able to touch Israel. Because God is going to war against these nations. God has weapons of mass destruction.

So let the wars begin! God will save his people; first God will bring a great earthquake to Israel he will make the earth feel like the ground is having convulsions. The army troops will not be able to stand on their feet. God will then make them confused and they will panic, because they will not be able to see from all the debris. The army troops will start killing each other because they cannot see what is in front of them.

Israel's enemies will die by friendly fire, and disease that God will put on them to render them in capable of attacking. Then to finish off the ones that are still alive, God will make it rain great hailstones, fire, and brimstones. The sky will rain with God's weapons of mass destruction until all the troops are dead. Listen people you do not want to go against God. So I say to you always stay in the light.

Welcome God

I welcome you my Lord, my God, my Almighty God, for none is greater than you. I invite you into my life; I invite you into my nation. We need you God today and always, come into our lives for without you our lives are like a scary movie. For we are sinners who need your guidance. In the name of Jesus, we ask for your forgiveness for our sins are like monsters with no home, or father to guide us.

Come into our nation and make us your people, for we have shut you out way to long, and would love to welcome you with open arms. We never wanted to reject you God, oh how we do miss you. My God please let your graces shine upon our nation, and forgive us for our sins. We have dismissed your glory, for our libraries no longer hold your words, Christmas carols no longer are song in public school. Easter vacation is replaced by spring break, and the Ten Commandments are no longer seen in public places.

Public places no longer praise your name. For our sins are great, and we ask for your forgiveness in Jesus name. We welcome and honor you always. Please come back to us my Lord my God.

What Did Jesus Say

John 12: 36 Jesus said, Believe in the light, so that you will be the people of the light.

John 14: 6 Jesus said, I am the way, the truth, and the life, no one goes to the Father except by me.

John 15: 20 if people persecuted me, they will persecute you too.

John 15: 18-19 Jesus said, if the world hates you, just remember that they hated me first. If you belong to the world, then the world will love you as its own. But if you do not belong to the world, but to me, the world will hate you.

John 15: 9-10 I love you just as the Father loves me, if you obey my commands, you will remain in my love, just as I have obeyed my Father's commands and remain in his love.

John 15: 12-16 Jesus said, his command is that you love one another, just as he loves us. The Father will give you whatever you ask of him in my name.

John 14: 1 Jesus said, there are many rooms in my Father's house, and I will prepare a place for you.

John 12: 25 Jesus said those who love their own life will lose it; those who hate their own life in this world will keep it for life eternal.

John 12: 26 whoever wants to serve me must follow me; so that my servant will be with me where I am. And my Father will honor anyone who serves me.

John 12: 48 Jesus said, the words I have spoken will be their Judge on the last day.

John 14: 23 Jesus said, those who love me will obey my teaching. My Father will love them, and my Father and I will come to them and live with them.

John 14: 13-14 if you ask me for anything in my name, I will do it.

There lots more were this came from. Read the Word and see what else Jesus said.

What Do God Want

God wants you to believe in the one he sent (John 6:29). Jesus said those who come to me will never be hungry. Those who believe in me will never be thirsty (John 6:35-39). Jesus will never turn away anyone who comes to him. If you go to Jesus he promises to raise you back to life on the last day. The Father said all who believe in the son shell have eternal life (John 6:40). John 6:63 tells us what gives life is Gods spirit.

If you want a spiritual life giving relationship with God, believe in his son Jesus Christ. Live by Gods law the Ten Commandments, live by his word his word is life. Do unto others as you would want them to do unto you. Love one another as the Lord loves you. Put God into your life on a daily basis. Believe and have faith in the son, who is your Lord and who loves you always. The love of God is a real love an eternal love for ever.

What Time Is It

Do you know the time? I was always saying the wars in the Middle East, is not our war. Why are we sending our people over there to fight? God has opened my eyes. I now know it is my war and your war. This war started 50 years after the death of Jesus Christ. The war to end all wars will be when all the nations gather against Jerusalem for the "Battle of Armageddon". This will be our last war.

Until then there will be many wars and rumors of wars, before the end arrives. The wars will get closer to gather and more destructive as the end of age approaches. It is by the grace of God that man has not destroyed himself yet. People think the war is over religion, but God put in my heart, that it is over the land he gave to his people, that he led, from Egypt into Israel. (Jeremiah 12:14-17) The Lord said as for all my wicked neighbors who seize the inheritance.

God gave the land to their fore fathers, Abraham, Isaac, and Jacob. The land belongs to the Jews. Israel is the clock God has given us, so we could tell what time it is. Gods plan revolves around the nation Israel (Jerusalem). When you want to know what time it is on Gods calendar or where we are on Gods plan, look at the clock; look at Israel and the Middle East. (Genesis 12:3) God told Abraham he would curse anyone who curses Israel.

In(Isaiah 54:4) God told Israel, do not be afraid, you will not be disgraced again, you will not be humiliated, your creator will be like a husband to you. When you see or hear Jerusalem being surrounded by armies of men, you will know Gods clock is working. (Matthew 24:6) The Palestinian leadership does not want peace with Israel. May the good Lord forgive them!

Peace negotiations have been going on for many years. People do not realize the significance of what is happening. (Genesis 19: 1-29).

What's Your Role

Very few of us understand the role we are playing in Gods great plan. Believe it or not some of us are here doing and saying things as part of Gods great plan. The same can be said for Satan. Some of us are here doing and saying things for the evil one. Remember that there are two Gods. God himself made Satan a god. Just too even things up. God the Son the Holy Spirit is one almighty God together. The almighty God will be the winner at the end of time.

God will take Satan out for good. By-by Satan. So as I have said once before pick your God. I know who my God is. Do you? As workers for God, we need to open man's eyes that they may turn themselves from darkness to light. Most Christian's eyes are open, but they have received nothing. They play and talk a good game. When a man is born again, he has received a gift from the almighty God. This gift will only get better in the Lords house.

Where Do You Belong

Every person on earth belongs to a kingdom. God's kingdom or Satan's kingdom.

God's kingdom will prevail. Satan's kingdom will be destroyed. So pick your kingdom.

How could they!
Jesus, how could they not love you?
How could they not believe?
How could they not have faith?
How could they not know?
How could they not see?
How could they not hear?
How could they!
How could they!

Jesus is God

Jesus was not a man, who became God. Jesus is God, who became a man. To make it possible for him to die. So he could pay the penalty for human sin. So sinners could be forgiven.

Christ humbled himself and became obedient to the point of death, even the death of the cross.

Jesus did all this for you and me. What will you do for him?

Where Will You Live

In (John 5: 24-29) Jesus said, those who hear my words and believe in me have already passed from death to life. Just as the Father is the source of life, so is Jesus the source of life. Jesus need only call your name from death and then you live. Your new life with Jesus, will be no more tears, there will be no more death, no more grief or pain (Revelation 21:4). All the evil, bad people of this world will have a second death. Our Lord will wake them also, but he will place them in the burning lake of fire and sulfur.

This is called the second death (Revelation 21:8). Now is the time to pick where you want to live, because you hold the key in your hand. There for your life is your choosing, there will be no one to blame only yourself. In our new home God will have nothing to do with impure or shameful things (Revelation 21:27). We are all being tested in this world, will you past your test? If Jesus is pleased with you, your name will be in his book of the living. So do your best to please our Lord, so we will meet in our new home.

Grace and truth come only through Jesus Christ, so open your arms and in brace the truth, the only truth. God bless Jesus Christ, and so shell we be blessed through Jesus, so let your light shine. When Jesus raises the dead to life, we will be immortal with spiritual bodies and other angel-like characteristics. Our new life will be totally different from anything in this earthly life. The word said we will not marry in heaven (Matthew 22: 29-33). We will be like angels, it will be impossible for us to die (Luke 20:36) we will live forever.

Because God is the God of the living not the dead. So then who is the God of the dead can you guest. Remember God will bless them, who come in the name of Jesus. Did you know God has two most important commandments he wants you to keep? Love the Lord your God with all your heart, with all your soul, with your entire mind, and with all your strength. His second most important commandment is to love your neighbor as you love yourself (Mark 12: 30). This means he wants you to learn to love each other.

Yes our God is all about love, so give him your love. Jesus is coming he will send his angels to gather his chosen people. Will he chose you? Jesus will set you free in his light, read (Matthew 24:30). Remember life is short, but our new life will last forever.

Who Are They

Has God left us, are we to corrupt? Can you blame him! We think we don't need God. We let Satan control us now. Who are the people of today? There is disrespect for parenthood, kids are now bringing them self's up, they are not being taught right from wrong. Parents say don't bother me, do what you want. Kids are growing up with no respect for their parents; their words to their parents are from Satan.

Today they know nothing of God or the bible. They have no respect about how past heroes fought for what they have today and they don't want to know. People are antifamily; they have no respect or even know the meaning of family. They now call their friends family, maybe this is why they need face book friends. Children of today are so rebellious because of their upbringing; they think they are grown at thirteen.

I find myself asking who are they, where did they come from It's like the earth was invaded with a different bread, a bread not of God. They have no respect for themselves anything of Satan goes. Do they even know who God is? Have they heard the name Jesus? They don't want to hear God's Words or your words; they were born smart so they say. They blame everyone else for their problems.

They do not understand why God do not bless them. I can just see a world full of sinners coming to invade the earth. My God have mercy on them. I can't help but to ask who they are. Where do they come from, are they of this world, are they of Satan, because I see no trace of God.

Who Can Open the Scroll

There is only one who is worthy to open God's scroll, the great descendant of David. The true king

Jesus Christ. Jesus will carry out his father's plan to the tee. God will send his seven spirits through all the whole earth. When I was reading about the seven seals, it sound like more clues about what will happen to earth. You should read Revelation 5, 6, 7, and 8, and see what you think.

Jesus has the key to the Kingdom of God. When Jesus opens a door, no one can close it. When he closes a door, no one can open it. Jesus can do this for you, if you stay in the light with your Lord. Jesus can keep you safe from your enemies; he can make your enemies bow down at your feet. So I say to you keep your faith in God and your Lord Jesus Christ.

Read Revelation 3: 7, Remember "Salvation" comes from our God and savior Jesus Christ. This is what and who you should put your faith in. A friend is here today and gone tomorrow. Jesus is always there. Jesus is your friend today, tomorrow, and always. Just open your heart and welcome him into your life.

Our Lord Jesus can make a change for you, always pray and repent your sins and sin no more. Our Lord is a forgiven God, but remember he is no fool!

Who DO You Work For

You are the salt of the earth. God made the earth for us to live on. He wants us to take care of it and keep it going. People should be proud in doing their jobs, because you are working for God first.

You are working for your boss second. If the salt losses its flavor, how should it be seasoned?

(Matthew 5:13-16) When people have no pride about their work, it will start to collapse. Then man will piece it back to gather over and over again until it disintegrates.

In the same since the earth starts to collapse and things keep getting patch back over and over again until it disintegrates. It is then good for nothing but to be thrown out and trampled over by man.

You are the light God put on this earth. Let your light shine. So everyone can see your good works. You are working in the name of Jesus. Let us all glorify our Father in heaven, for putting us here to work for him.

Your talent and skills are your light from God. Both small and large, no matter the size of skill. Give light to the world, the light of our God. For God gave each person light to shine in his world. Do not turn off the lamp. Let it shine; let it out shine the darkness.

Who Is the Antichrist

Who is the Antichrist? This is a question everyone would like to know. All God tells us is that he may come from Europe. The Antichrist will come because of the world's chaos, when the world's instability and disorder cause a worldwide out cry for relief, and order from the chaos in the world. This will set the stage for a new world leader. This leader will promise a solution to all the world's problems.

This leader will promise order and security, plus world peace, everyone will be taken with this new leader, people will love him, and put him over the whole world. The Antichrist is introduced and described in detail in the bible. Please read (1John 2:18, 22, 4:3) and read (2John 7). Then the bible talks about the Antichrist under various aliases names. So please read (Daniel 9:26 NKJV) were he is called the prince who is to come.

Please, please do not mix this up with Jesus who is to come. Remember the Antichrist likes to copy Jesus. Read (Daniel 8:23 NKJV) he is called a fierce king. In (Daniel 8:23 NIV) he is called a master of intrigue. Read (Daniel 11:21 NLT) he is called a despicable man. In (Zechariah 11:16-17 NLT) he is called a worthless shepherd. Read (2 Thessalonians 2:3 NLT) he is called the one who brings destruction.

Read (2 Thessalonians 2:8 NKJV) he is called the lawless one. Then in (2: Thessalonians 2:9 NLT) he is the evil man. And in (Revelation 13:1 NKJV) he is called the beast. This global leader, the Antichrist is a person who is against Jesus Christ; he will openly oppose Jesus and say he is Jesus. The Antichrist is Satan's number one man. The Antichrist persecutes tortures and kills all people who are for God. He will aggressively live up to his name the Antichrist.

In (Revelation 13:18 NIV) tells us if you are wise and intelligent you can figure out the meaning of the number 666, because that number stand for someone's name. Some of you may ask, why God didn't just tell us the name. I'm sure you all know that answer. I say to you take to heart when Jesus tell you to keep watching and be aware. Because the Antichrist knows human nature, he knows how to dazzle and gratify your craving for things of this world, do not let him into your sole, stay in the light.

Why Armageddon

It is God's plan to cut the chain from his people the Jews. They have rejected their Messiah time after time. God gave chance after chance to return to him and they still rejected him, (Jeremiah 30:8-11). God said he will break their chains, and they will serve him and King Jesus. God will gather all the nations together, for the last war Armageddon. God will destroy all who do not believe in his son Jesus.

But he will not destroy his people of Israel, so they should not be afraid, God said he will save his people. Have faith your God has not forgotten you, for he cares for his people (Jeremiah 30:14-18). God said he attacked you like an enemy he gave you a harsh punishment, because your sins were great. But now he will take all your enemies away. Have faith and trust in your God for he will rebuild Jerusalem and restore its palace.

Please read (Jeremiah 30:21:24) For God is for you his people. Your ruler will come from your nation; your prince will come from your own people. Know that your God has always loved you and always will. God only wants to be your God and you to be his people. So believe, trust and have faith. For peace is due to the entire world. Armageddon will be the last war around the end of the Tribulation period.

Were all the nation will meet in the" Valley of Judgment. "In (Joel 3:14-15) tells us that it is there that the day of the Lord will soon come. On that day the sun and the moon will grow dark, and the stars will no longer shine. The Valley of Judgment is the Mountain of Megiddo. Located in northern Israel starting at the Mediterranean Sea, another name for this mountain is "Mount of Slaughter".

This war will end all wars for a New Kingdom is to come. A Kingdom of peace and love, a Kingdom without sin. Our Lord and God will live among us and we shall praise his name.

Wicked People

Wicked people believe God do not see or hear them. The wicked give arrogant orders and even God's people turn to them and believe whatever they say. They speak evil of God and think God will not know. But God see and hear everything. God will make the wicked fall to destruction. I say to you do not be jealous of the wicked because you think everything goes well for them, when their hearts pour out evil and their minds are busy with wicked schemes.

God is good to those who have pure hearts, so don't let them steel your faith. The wicked laugh at other people and speak of evil things. They make plans to oppress others and trick you into joining them in their evil ways. It may seem to you that the wicked have plenty and is always getting more, know that this is the work of Satan he wants to keep you happy so you will stay in his control. I tell you now stay in the light of Jesus and all your needs will be given to you in Jesus name.

God has set a time for judgment and he will judge fair. God will make those who are unfaithful and ugly to you pay for all your sorrows. So hold your head high and you will survive. Those who are evil will not survive God's judgment. Those who are righteous will live because they are faithful to God. Evil does not grow in the soil, nor does trouble grow out of the ground, we bring trouble on ourselves (Job 5: 6-8). Beware there are people who live for trouble, just to bring you down in the dark so beware.

In Habakkuk 2:4 God said those who are evil will not survive, but those who are righteous will live, because they are faithful to God. Our Lord our God is telling us that the righteous will live again in his kingdom, because they have been faithful to him through all their sorrows. And the evil wicked ones will not survive to live again in his kingdom. The wicked will go to the wicked one, to burn in a pit of fire forever.

In Habakkuk 2:5 tells us greedy people are proud and restless, they are never satisfied and their restlessness makes them deceitful, they taunt others to make themselves feel good. But what the wicked don't know is that in the Lord's book they are doomed never to live again. So I say to all the righteous, hold your ground and keep your faith, because your life will be paradise. Just stay in the light with Jesus.

Will They Change

Jesus will start to deal with man's rebellion on earth during the Tribulation period. Every creature will be judged, from the days of Adam to the rapture. Praise and worship are due the Father and the Son throughout all eternity. Before the second coming, our Father will give people time to accept Jesus as Messiah. Then their fate is sealed forever. Jesus is in charge of the judgments and their timing. All should honor the son just as they honor the Father.

As time go on war will escalate, war will rule the whole world. Wars of foolish and deceitful men will kill farmers, destroy land, and crops, and cause the collapse of social, physical and political structures; these wicked men will destroy, confiscate and hoard food supplies, causing despair, misery, poverty, and death. There will be a great economic, disaster, and famine. Food will sell for ridiculously high price.

Just a small quart of food will cost the equivalent of a day's wages. No money will be left for clothes, housing or automobiles. Many will not be able to survive this. As always the sinful people will take advantage of disasters. The picture will be gloomy. A worldwide economic disaster will occur.

Things will grow progressively worse. Evil men and imposters will grow worse. So will economic collapse and famine. Think about it with not enough food in the world. The animals will turn on man for their food.

There will be plagues, starvation, diseases, etc. This is the eternal domination of more than one billion people. There will be a great earthquake that will shake the whole world. It will be massive. Things from the sky will fall on us. Mountains and islands will move out of its place. Humanity must make a moral about face. There will be worldwide panic. The basic necessities of life will be scarce. Multitudes will admit the existence of God. But will they change?

Everyone will have the opportunity to accept salvation before they die, or take the mark of the beast. God's wrath will destroy one third of the earth and sea. The grace of God will allow two thirds of the earth more time. Will they change? When one third of the earth's fresh water supply is contaminated, and they watch each other die from thirst, and others die from drinking the tainted water. Will they change?

As we go on living our life without Jesus. There will be a reduction in the earth's sunlight. This will affect the weather, crops, and all of life in general. Major winter storms will sweep the earth, causing multitudes of people to freeze to death. The remaining on earth will persist in their sin, refusing to repent, and continuing to reject Jesus. Demon worship will be worldwide. Man will have a Satanic Bible that will be widely read.

And the church of Satan will be filled. Multitudes will bow before statues and images of the Antichrist. They will soon learn what happens to those who forget God. So I ask again will they change. Our fate is in that question. Will they change? Our Father gives us years and years to change. Will they change? I myself think God already knows the answer. Our fate is written in his book. But his good grace is still waiting to see if we will change. In the name of Jesus I pray.

Will We Lose Faith

There is so much sin in the world today. People know sin comes from the evil one. But they do not try or want to fight the evil away. They just let the evil take over their minds and body. There is a rejection of God's truth, a falling away from their Lord. As time goes on this rejection, will become greater and greater. They are turning their ears away from the truth, the truth is Jesus. Today is our time to proclaim the grace of God because we are here by Gods good grace.

The Lord Jesus is our salvation by God's grace the Holy Spirit. Our souls will be saved by trusting and believing in Jesus Christ. The Rapture will come when people no longer believe in our Lord, and there will be a widespread rejection of God and people will fall from the faith. This rejection of God will be worldwide and our Lord God will take his Holy Spirit and grace from the earth, and he will no longer protect us.

Rejecting God will also open the door for the Antichrist, and then earth will truly be hell. Then we will beg God to save us once more, but this time it will be different. This time it will be the "Day of the Lord." A day of divine judgment upon the world. This day is the day when the Lord returns. May God have mercy upon our souls.

World Chaos

The world's chaos will increase as we approach the end of this age. Just before these tensions explode into world chaos, God will rapture his church and depopulate much of the earth. People will suddenly disappear from the world. God will take his believer's to heaven, before the Antichrist comes. But all of Christ new converts will still be here on earth with the Antichrist. This is a good reason to stay in the light.

People may be thinking one man cannot rule a whole world, I too would think this if not for technology. We are setting things up today to make it easy for the Antichrist. How about instant global communication, the internet, satellite cell phones, air transportation, web site's like face book, that will be able to keep track with all the people on earth, and global news like CNN is seen everywhere in the world.

When the Antichrist comes he would just have to sit at the middle of the world, and push buttons to see and get what he needs. With all the new technology people are being traced, and all their information is just a push of a button. Some web site's today already know where you are, and where you go, who your friends are, who your kin are, where you work, and where you play, think about it!

The world wants you to share everything about yourself. I now here things about microchips. The same Implants that they put under a dogs skin, so they can track them when they are lost. Microchips will be surgically implanted under people skin at birth. These chips will be loaded with information about you. What I can't figure out is how they would upgrade your info. May be you have some ideals! This is good reason to stay in the light.

Year of God's Power

Some people think the year 2012 calls for the end of time. But I know better because no man knows when the end will come, only God knows this. There are signs that point to the year 2012, but I believe these signs mark 2012 as a year of great tragedy. I believe we will have a series of bad weather and hard times and or things that only the Lord knows about. I believe this will be a year that God will show us he is in control of all things.

Our Lord is telling us to wake up and come to him, for he is your God he wants you to be his people and live in Jesus Kingdom to come. Come live with the Son of God Jesus Christ, now is the time to call on Jesus. For the light of Jesus is waiting for you, let Jesus take your hand and lead your way, for his light shines for you. The time is now to be washed with his light, let his light shower you with his blessings.

People are walking around thinking they are more than what they are. This is the year God will show you that you are nothing without him. You may think you don't need God, because you have your home, family, friends, and your job. You think you made it were you are on your own will, I say you need to rethink, because your God put you there. And the Lord can take it away, and make you crawl again.

For he is your Lord and God and he can blow your house down. I think the year 2012 will show us more of God's power before it's over, people will wish for this year to pass quick. But our Lord my extend his will another year, because we are stubborn people, because we are people who do not like the light of Jesus. God will show his power this year, so run to Jesus for his blessing and stay in the light.

Your Choice

God said I have given you a choice between a blessing and a curse (Deuteronomy 30: 1). If you do right by God he will have mercy on you when you repent unto him. And he will bring his blessing to you. God oppressed the people who were against his people. So never worry about what people think or say against you. When you love your Lord, he we make you prosperous in all that you do in Jesus name.

When your enemies try to bring you down. The Lord will make you prosperous to show your enemies he is your God. This is God's way of saying to your enemies don't miss with my people. That's why you need to turn to God with all your heart, he is a real friend your only true friend. Put your trust in the Lord. God gave you a choice between good and evil. God gave you a choice between life and death (Deuteronomy 30: 15-20). God gave you the mind to know right from wrong.

You cannot change others and you do not have to follow other people evil ways. If you need someone to follow, follow Jesus. You can make your own choice don't let others chose for you, they will lead you to the evil one. You have the choice of God's blessing or God's curse. Be faithful to your Lord, because you have the choice between life and death.

Your life is not over until God say it is over, he can renew your life in the Kingdom of God. I say to you stay in the light and look for your Lord Jesus Christ. He is not far you have only to open the door. Seek and you shell find, he is there for you to find and let him into your heart. You have the choice to live with Jesus. So I say again stay in Jesus light.

Reference

Good News Translation (GNT)

Holman Illustrated Bible Dictionary

NIV

NKJV

NLT

About the Author

Times are changing the world seem to be going in the wrong direction. People are having very hard times, and I want to give some hope to people through my book "Stay in the Light". People are losing hope, they are losing their jobs, people are worried about how to feed their families, and how to keep a roof over their head.

People are losing their self-worth for themselves and others. The world needs help, and I pray the words in "Stay in the Light" will give them hope. I had twenty seven years on my job, and it was out sourced I had to take early retirement. I found myself out looking for a job.

I did find a couple of short term jobs, after that I could not find anything. I now just put my trust in our Lord and he carries me through day to day. I thank our Lord for my blessing. I live in the state of Michigan, and things here are slow.

But I never give up for myself or for others, because we do have a savior we can call on. May he who is coming bless our nation.